"How can Christians live faithfully w[...]ive or too complacent? Is there a middle grou[...]warm but rather is alive with a radically normal devotion to Christ? In this provocative and timely book, pastor Josh Kelley suggests that the most radical pursuit of Christ has more to do with joyfully leaning into grace than it does with being a self-sufficient Super Christian. It's fashionable today to be radical, to subvert the safe patterns of middle-class Christianity. But truly radical Christianity may not be what you think it is. Embracing God's call wherever God has placed us is the most radical thing we can do."

Brett McCracken
author of *Hipster Christianity: When Church and Cool Collide*
and *Gray Matters: Navigating the Space Between Legalism and Liberty*

"Through his biblical insight, humor, and humility, Josh Kelley assures us that we can be committed Christ followers without being kooky or uptight. *Radically Normal* is an enjoyable and refreshing read for every new believer, seasoned Christian, or burned-out ministry worker who needs to be reminded that our everyday lives can be exciting and meaningful when we follow Jesus wholeheartedly."

Cindi McMenamin
national speaker and author of *When Women Walk Alone*

"If you'd like help on living for Jesus in a way that's so surprisingly different from either legalism or complacency that it has to be called radical, then Josh Kelley's *Radically Normal* should be in your hands right now."

Robert H. Mounce
Biblical scholar and translator
president emeritus, Whitworth University

"Greatness is all about being great in the eyes of God. But understanding God's mission, regardless of who you are, can be a challenge. In a very entertaining way, Josh Kelley's book helped me to better understand what kind of Christian God has called me to be."

Jake Byrne
tight end for the NFL's San Diego Chargers

"In this delightful book, Josh Kelley clearly identifies two extremes we see every day in the church—obsessive Christianity and complacent Christianity. He offers insightful and sometimes humorous illustrations and stories to show what these extremes look like, and he offers solid, biblical advice on how to reach a radically normal balance. This book will help you find that balance in your life."

Rick Walston
president, Columbia Evangelical Seminary

"If you've ever felt lost in the Christian chatter about living too radically or too complacently, then *Radically Normal* is for you. Josh Kelley's skillfully written book will help you move past your guilt—or your obsessive tendencies—and discover a joy-driven, obedient life that gets kingdom work done."

Caleb Breakey
author of *Called to Stay* and *Dating Like Airplanes*

"I have always wanted to be radically normal—I just didn't have the right name or a well-considered definition. Now I have both. Read, learn, and inwardly digest...and be ready to pass it on!"

Graham Kerr
international television personality
award-winning author of 29 books

"In *Radically Normal*, my friend Josh Kelley cleverly dismantles the either/or thinking that causes us to live half-lives halfheartedly. Having spent the seminal years of my own life struggling to be as 'spiritual' Monday through Saturday as I was on Sunday, I'm thankful that God helped me see the exciting, enjoyable, everyday possibilities of normal Christianity. To experience God in everything is to enjoy a much greater view of spirituality, and my hat is off to Josh for handing out God-colored glasses to everyone!"

Dave Browning
lead pastor, Christ the King Community Church
author of *Deliberate Simplicity*

"*Radically Normal* completely resonated with me, a Christian who has run the church gamut, encountering hand-clapping Charismatics, head-bowing solemn worshippers, and zealous missionaries. Comparing myself to all types of Christians, I've questioned my faith, often doubting I was radical enough. Josh's engaging style makes *Radically Normal* a fun, enlightening read that affirmed my place in the kingdom of God as a radically normal Christian."

Holly Michael
author and journalist

RADICALLY

NORMAL

Josh Kelley

HARVEST HOUSE PUBLISHERS
EUGENE, OREGON

Except where noted, Scripture quotations are taken from the Holy Bible, New International Version®, NIV®. Copyright © 1973, 1978, 1984, 2011 by Biblica, Inc.® Used by permission. All rights reserved worldwide.

Verses marked NRSV are from the New Revised Standard Version of the Bible, copyright © 1989 by the Division of Christian Education of the National Council of the Churches of Christ in the USA. Used by permission. All rights reserved.

Verses marked ESV are from The ESV® Bible (The Holy Bible, English Standard Version®), copyright © 2001 by Crossway, a publishing ministry of Good News Publishers. Used by permission. All rights reserved.

Verses marked KJV are from the King James Version of the Bible.

Cover by Harvest House Publishers, Inc., Eugene, Oregon

Back cover author photo by Jason Weigner

RADICALLY NORMAL
Copyright © 2014 by Joshua C. Kelley
Published by Harvest House Publishers
Eugene, Oregon 97402
www.harvesthousepublishers.com

Library of Congress Cataloging-in-Publication Data
    Kelley, Josh, 1973-
    Radically normal / Josh Kelley.
      pages cm
    Includes bibliographical references.
    ISBN 978-0-7369-5938-4 (pbk.)
    ISBN 978-0-7369-5939-1 (eBook)
    1. Christian life. I. Title.
    BV4501.3.K4455 2014
    248.4—dc23

2013048207

All rights reserved. No part of this publication may be reproduced, stored in a retrieval system, or transmitted in any form or by any means—electronic, mechanical, digital, photocopy, recording, or any other—except for brief quotations in printed reviews, without the prior permission of the publisher.

Printed in the United States of America

14 15 16 17 18 19 20 21 22 / VP-CD / 10 9 8 7 6 5 4 3 2 1

To the two people most responsible for this book...

Marilyn Kelley—from raising a family, to serving in ministry, to writing this book, we are on the same team.

Brother Jack, C.S. Lewis—as you once said of George MacDonald, now I say of you, "I have never concealed the fact that I regarded him as my master; indeed I fancy I have never written [anything] in which I did not quote from him."

Acknowledgments

I owe many people debts of gratitude. I hope I don't forget too many.

To my family—my wife, Marilyn, for believing I could do this, and our daughters, Grace and Sarah, for filling my life with joy. To my parents, who demonstrated God's unconditional love. The longer I live the more I realize how great and rare that gift was. Thank you to all of the family members who supported us in so many ways during the writing of the book.

To my church, the Gathering, I owe a particularly large debt. I couldn't have done this without you. Thank you for being such a loving and supportive community. You're my glory and joy.

I also owe a great debt to my first church, His Place. Serving with you has been one of my greatest privileges. Only God knew how he was using you to prepare me for this book. "Red ink equals love" sustained me through the editing process.

Thank you to the Skagit Starbucks. I'm proud to have been a partner with you and hope you enjoy these stories. To the Mount Vernon Haggen Starbucks, where I did most of my writing, thank you for providing such a welcoming second office.

Thank you to many friends who have been such an important part of my journey. I owe so much to so many that I am afraid to even begin listing them. I have to limit my thanks here to Jon and Rachelle Brown and Nate and Heather Baker, who supported us and this book so much.

Thank you to my proofreaders: Mom and Dad, Aunt Terri, Rachelle Brown, Gretchen Cohen, Pam David, Brian and Susanna Heinze, Scott and Jacqueline Hendrickson, Dan Holland, Michel Jevons, Israel Kloss, Leslie McDaniels, Cheryl Neff, Marian Orange, Christian Overman, Denise Skelton, Joy Steem, Matthew Steem, Nellie Strong, Tiffany Watkins, and Karen Westra. Special thanks to Cheryl Lanahan, Nate and Heather Baker, and Bruce Wersen for invaluable input when the book was still very rough, and to Kyle Dillon, who provided a scholar's perspective. Above all, thank you to Cheryle Coapstick, whose brutal edits on the earliest drafts prevented this from becoming a dry treatise.

Thank you to my publisher, Harvest House, for taking a chance on me. I'm truly fortunate to be with such a warm and supportive team. Special thanks to Terry Glaspey, the acquisitions editor who championed my book and helped others catch the vision, and to Gene Skinner, whose work and guidance made this a better book.

Simply acknowledging God seems to trivialize my complete dependency on him. He's the very soul, inspiration, purpose, and hope of this book. Instead, I will just sign,

To the glory of God and the joy of the saints!

Josh

Contents

A Note to the Reader

I wrote this book assuming that most of my readers would be Christians and familiar with evangelicalism. If you aren't, I'm delighted to have you read it—maybe it will help you see Christianity in a new light. Please forgive me if some references don't quite make sense.

All the stories in this book are true to the best of my recollection. In some cases I changed nonessential details in order to obscure the identities of individuals.

My stories might give you the impression that I grew up in a legalistic church or a strict family. Nothing could be further from the truth. I grew up in a loving family and attended a great church. Granted, they were both a little quirky in their own way, but I couldn't have asked for a better home or home church. The self-righteousness I struggle with springs from my own heart.

Finally, I didn't write this book as a response to any other book or author (even the title was created well before I read a similarly titled book). Rather, I wrote this book to correct a large assortment of ideas and practices, some of which have been around since the early church. For that reason, and because I prize the unity of the body of Christ, I avoided naming specific books and authors I disagree with. If you're dying to know, I'm sure you'll be able to figure it out with a little research.

There is no use trying to be more spiritual than God. God never meant man to be a purely spiritual creature. That is why He uses material things like bread and wine to put the new life into us. We may think this rather crude and unspiritual. God does not: He invented eating. He likes matter. He invented it.

C.S. Lewis, *Mere Christianity*

Obsessive and Complacent Christianity

Starbucks is a big part of my life. I hold most of my meetings at Starbucks and write my sermons there. I have my monthly father-daughter dates at Starbucks. I'm at Starbucks as I write this. But in the spring of 2011, I had no idea the role Starbucks would play in my story.

I had been an assistant pastor at one of the biggest churches in Skagit Valley (about an hour north of Seattle). When I became the lead pastor of one of the smallest churches in the area, I was filled with dreams of all I'd do. In the first three and a half years, I grew the Gathering from about 100 people to about 75—not the sort of thing that one brags about at pastors' conventions.

This is the story of the lessons God taught me through Starbucks over the next 18 months. It's also the book I wish I had when I was growing up. All the books I read back then seemed to imply that following God with my whole heart meant enjoying this life less and less.

This book tells how I discovered that the opposite is true.

Going to Extremes

One day when I was about ten years old, my family arrived early at our pastor's house for a Bible study, and I saw Pastor Arnie sitting in front of the TV watching a football game. Apparently, his team wasn't doing well, because he was kind of grumpy and was shouting quietly at the TV. "What? Come on! Are you blind?"

Seeing my pastor watch football was unsettling, but I wasn't sure why. I didn't think TV was wrong (I watched *Star Blazers* every morning before school), and I didn't have a problem with football (my mom loves football). But it seemed so unspiritual. In my ten-year-old logic, I assumed my pastor must do only spiritual stuff.

We're haunted by the feeling that God must be happier when we read our Bibles than when we watch football.

So many of us have a deep-seated fear that we have to choose—do we want to be obsessive Christians who don't enjoy this life, or do we want to be complacent Christians who have a lot of fun here? We feel as if those are our only two options. Should we give up football, sell all of our possessions, and become missionaries to India? Or should we have nice houses, be well liked, and climb the corporate ladder? We know those aren't really the only options, but we're still haunted by the feeling that God must be happier when we read our Bibles than when we watch football. I wonder how many Christians remain lukewarm primarily because they think that being on fire would be miserable.

As we journey along the path of our Christian life, we hear sermons and read books that warn us about a dangerous cliff called complacency. And for good reason—the distractions of this life are constantly pulling us away from God. But I'm becoming more and more aware of another cliff on the other side of the path. That cliff is called obsession, and it's just as dangerous as complacency. Obsession isn't about loving Jesus, but trying to look like a really good Christian.

In our human sinfulness, we tend to be proud of our obsessiveness or to excuse our complacency. But the life that God desires isn't found at either extreme. Wholehearted devotion to God consists of radical obedience lived out in surprisingly normal, joy-filled ways. This is what I mean by being radically normal. It's the biblical art of fully engaging this life while focusing on the next.

The Problem with Complacency

My wife, Marilyn, grew up in a blurry world. She was so nearsighted she couldn't read the blackboard at school, causing her schoolwork to suffer. She didn't know she was nearsighted—she thought that was what the world was supposed to look like. When Marilyn was seven, she got her first pair of glasses. It was like heaven opened up and shone its light on the earth. Until that moment, she didn't know that trees were covered with individual leaves or that the teacher had been writing actual words on the blackboard.

I think most Christians are spiritually nearsighted. We see the things right in front of us—food and drink, relationships, clothes, books, work, vacations—with crystal clarity. But prayer, worship, sacrifice, righteousness, heaven, and even God himself are often out of focus and hazy. This isn't necessarily our fault, just as Marilyn's nearsightedness wasn't her fault. It's part of our common condition as creatures of flesh and blood. But how will we respond to our nearsightedness? Complacent Christians are happy to stay nearsighted. They're content focusing on the things right in front of their noses and keeping unseen realities at arm's length, in the blurry zone.

The problem with complacent Christianity is its mediocrity. In the movie *Good Will Hunting*, Will is an Einstein-level genius who seems to be content working blue-collar jobs. As Will deals with his past, he must choose to embrace his potential. In one scene, Will tells his best friend, Chuckie, that he's looking forward to working in construction and watching Patriots games for the rest of his life. Here's Chuckie's response.

> Look, you're my best friend, so don't take this the wrong way. In twenty years, if you're still livin' here, comin' over to my house to watch the Patriots' games, still workin' construction, I'll [blanking] kill you. That's not a threat, now. That's a fact. I'll [blanking] kill you.

Chuckie knows that Will is settling for far too little. Each day that Will spends in construction is a day he's wasting. That is exactly how I feel about complacent Christianity (without the swearing)—not that complacency is too sinful or too worldly but that it's too dull, too meaningless, too little. It's far below what we were meant for. My favorite author, C.S. Lewis, described it this way.

> We are half-hearted creatures, fooling around with drink and sex and ambition when infinite joy is offered us, like an ignorant child who wants to go on making mud pies in a slum because he cannot imagine what is meant by the offer of a holiday at the sea. We are far too easily pleased.[1]

I've seen my share of lukewarm, half-committed, self-serving, near-sighted Christians. They spend their money on immediate thrills, work harder for praise from man than praise from God, leave their spouses when marriage gets too hard, and give little thought to life outside of their own little bubble. When I observe complacent Christians, I don't feel indignation; I feel pity. They are far too easily pleased.

The Problem with Obsession

Many pastors and Christian authors try to correct complacent Christianity by promoting obsessive Christianity. In effect, they say, "Stop focusing so much on the things of this life!" Their antidote to nearsightedness is farsightedness. Obsessive Christians don't say earthly stuff is evil, but they hint that the more you focus on God, the blurrier this life should become.

These folks remind me of a Christian teacher I once knew. She had really bad eyesight but believed that God told her not to wear glasses. I think the idea was that leaving her glasses at home made her depend more on him. I can't comment on whether she heard God correctly— that's none of my business. But I do know she complained of frequent headaches and looked odd. The perpetual squinting gave her a mole-like appearance.

Obsessive Christians might say the rest of us are nearsighted and unable to see God clearly because we're not squinting enough. We're not giving enough, serving enough, praying enough, sacrificing enough. They might tell us to spurn the pleasures of life, hate the world, and stop getting caught up in earthly things. Do all that, and *then* you'll gain spiritual focus. *Then* you'll start enjoying a four-hour worship service more than a trip to Disneyland. You'll be perfectly happy to sell your possessions and move to India.

Many of us who hear their advice feel guilty for not doing enough to focus on God. We wonder if something is wrong with us. But trying to follow their advice isn't the answer—it leaves us looking as odd and unapproachable as that squinting mole-teacher looked to me.

Too many Christians struggle under the weight of trying to do enough. They're so busy trying to be spiritual enough that they miss God's blessings in everyday life. They're like frightened children who refuse to go to the beach because they think their father would be more pleased if they did extra chores.

Worse yet, I've watched some Christians break under the strain of spiritual farsightedness and walk away from God completely. As we'll later see, the Bible teaches that God created us for joy—not just in heaven someday, but here and now. Here's the thing. If you believe you can't find joy with God, you'll try to find it without him. Or you'll try to squelch your longing for joy, and your soul will shrivel. That's one reason why we see so many withered, sour Christians in the world.

> **If you believe you can't find joy with God, you'll try to find it without him.**

I wonder how many atheists were once obsessive Christians who hoped their joyless faith wasn't true. That is basically C.S. Lewis's story. As a young man, he wanted to be free of the drudgery of his childhood faith long before he rejected God for rational reasons. Ultimately it was joy that brought him back to God.[2] Do you know anyone who walked away from God because he or she couldn't find happiness in the church? Could you be heading in that direction?

Another Option

In the parable of the prodigal son (Luke 15:11-31), the prodigal son starts out looking a lot like complacent, nearsighted Christians. He wanted his inheritance so he could leave his father and blow it all in wild living. Complacent Christians want God's blessings—life, money, food, possession, sex—but want him to stay safely out of focus so they can use those things however they want. When they use God's good gifts in sinful, destructive ways, they end up suffering the consequences.

The prodigal's older brother reminds me of obsessive, farsighted Christians. His father has to remind him, "Everything I have is yours." Obsessive Christians are squinting so hard that they can't enjoy the Father's gifts right under their noses. Is it any surprise they doubt his goodness? The parable showcases God's forgiveness and acceptance of the lost, but it also teaches us how easily we can be separated from God without even leaving home.

Obsessive Christians can keep squinting for a long time without realizing how distant from God they are.

If I had to choose one of those options, I'd rather be complacent than obsessive. Does that surprise you? Complacent Christianity will prove itself empty enough when the famine comes. Sitting in the pigpen, the prodigal son quickly realized how unfulfilling his life actually was. His misery sent him back to his father. In contrast, Jesus leaves us wondering what the older brother will decide to do. Will he embrace the father's joy and grace and join the party, or will he remain outside, sullen and angry? Obsessive Christians can keep squinting for a long time without realizing how distant from God they are.

Fortunately, those are not the only options. Between the extremes of obsessive and complacent Christianity lies what I'm calling radically normal Christianity. This isn't a novel idea I dreamed up—I'm simply putting a name to what the Bible has always taught. I want to show you just how much the Bible has to say about being radically committed to God in perfectly normal ways, about discovering a clear-sighted faith that shares God's delight in both earthly and spiritual things.

Our Father

Years ago, before Marilyn and I had children, we visited Israel. Walking through the Old City of Jerusalem one afternoon, we saw a little Jewish boy trotting behind his father, struggling to keep pace. As he fell behind, I heard him shout, "Abba! Abba!" and then the dad slowed down so his son could catch up. As I watched them walk off hand in hand, I realized I had just experienced the most profound lesson of the entire trip. I had studied the Greek New Testament and dissected complicated passages, but now I finally understood the words "And by him we cry, 'Abba, Father'" (Romans 8:15) in a way that my commentaries failed to convey. Sometimes we forget that *Father* is not simply a name for God—it is a profound revelation of his relationship with us.

Now a father myself, every day that I spend with my daughters teaches me more about my heavenly Father. My little girls, Grace and Sarah, are exactly 21 months apart. Sometimes I wonder how we got through their first few years without going insane or getting divorced. But we survived, and now I absolutely love being the daddy of two little girls. It's what I was meant for. I don't need a son to play catch with (I don't even like catch). I'm much happier reading The Chronicles of Narnia to them or going on our father-daughter dates.

One of my favorite parts of being a daddy is simply watching Grace and Sarah play. They build fairy houses in the backyard and make soup for the fairies out of grass clippings and rose petals. When it rains (as it often does in Washington), they come inside and turn their beds into a fort and fill it with stuffed animals. Few things give me more joy than listening to their make-believe adventures. Today, they told me that their stuffed animals had to go to jail for stealing candy while they were sleepwalking. I have no idea where they come up with this stuff.

It's one thing to know God loves me, but it's another altogether to delight in my children and marvel at how much more God must delight in me. I think of how much I enjoy watching my daughters play, and I wonder how much more God must enjoy watching us play in this world he has given us.

We forget that this world is good stuff. When God finished creating it, he didn't say, "This isn't half bad for my first try, but I hope they don't enjoy it too much." He said it was very good. Then 2000 years ago, he become one of us and lived in it himself. While Jesus was here, he prayed, worshipped, read the Bible, and fed the poor, but he also feasted, drank, slept, laughed, cried, and told jokes.

I know that being a father isn't all play. My role includes making sure Grace and Sarah put their beds back together, empty the dishwasher, and do their homework. Disciplining and teaching are absolutely vital, but those aren't my favorite parts of being a daddy. Likewise, I know that God's highest desire for us is eternal joy, and sometimes that means we must experience discipline and suffering. Yet Scripture hints that God is happiest when he can give us both earthly and spiritual joy.

> God is happiest when he can give us both earthly and spiritual joy.

It's Better Than You'd Hoped

My parents are from Southern California, but we moved to Washington State when I was three. Every couple years we'd go back to visit my grandparents. My dad hated wasting money on motels, so we'd leave as soon as he got off work and drive straight through the night. My parents laid blankets out for my brother, sister, and me in the back of our Datsun B-210, and we slept for the first part of the trip (this was before seat belt laws). For me, summer vacation officially began as I dozed off, looking at the stars out the hatchback window. But the highlight of every trip was Disneyland. Regardless of how tight money was, my parents always managed to take us to "the happiest place on earth." Not surprisingly, Disneyland has always held a special place in my heart.

As Marilyn and I watched Grace and Sarah fall in love with fairies and princesses, we became more and more eager to share the magic of Disneyland with them. We decided the ideal age would be when Sarah was seven and Grace nine—old enough to really enjoy and remember it but young enough to experience the wonder. The problem was that the money just wasn't there, so for two or three years, we prayed that God would provide a way. Almost every night, as I watched my little princesses sleep, I'd silently pray, "Father, I know that a trip to Disneyland isn't the most important thing in the world, but please, please make a way for us to take our little girls there."

Sometimes God's answers to the seemingly frivolous prayers mean the most. I don't know where all the money came from, but between pinching pennies, using air miles, and finding amazing deals, we were able to book the trip as part of a visit to my sister and her family, who are missionaries in Mexico. Circumstances beyond our control dictated that we'd arrive on Sarah's birthday, so they would still be seven and nine (at least until 8:23 p.m., when Sarah would turn eight).

Of course, we couldn't just tell our girls they were going to Disneyland. The telling had to be an event. We sat Grace and Sarah on the couch and gave them packages containing Minnie Mouse ears and Disneyland T-shirts. "When we go to California to visit Great-Grandpa," Marilyn said, "we're taking you to a very special place. Those presents are your clues."

We waited eagerly for the squeals of excitement as they opened the packages. Instead, they just stared at the gifts. Silence. Off in the distance, my neighbor was mowing his lawn.

"Where do you think we're going?" I finally asked.

"Well, it has to do with Disneyland," Grace said.

"Yes…it has to do with Disneyland," I said. "Where do you think we're going that has to do with Disneyland?"

"We don't know."

"Guess. It has to do with *Disneyland.*"

"We don't know!"

This was not going according to plan. Trying not to feel disappointed, we tried again. "It's in California and has to do with Disneyland. Where could that be?"

"We don't know!" Grace said.

"Just tell us!" begged Sarah.

Finally I gave in. "We're going to Disneyland!"

Grace started squealing, and Sarah got very quiet, as she does when she's especially excited. We had a great time telling them all about the rides and showing them pictures of Disneyland. But all the while, I thought about their anticlimactic response to the Minnie Mouse ears.

I didn't have to wait too long to find out what was really going on. Grace told my wife they knew immediately we meant Disneyland but were afraid to say it out loud in case they were wrong. They were afraid to even hope for something that good. I lack the words to describe how that affected me. I can only say that parenthood is filled with moments of sweet heartbreak, like when they break their favorite toy or finally toss out their tattered blankie.

Their innocence and lack of presumption were beautiful. They had received a gift they didn't expect and were afraid to embrace it. But I was also heartbroken. Didn't they know we'd do anything we could for them? That they were worth a trip to Disneyland and so much more? Had we been talking too much about how tight money was?

Over the next few days, that scene kept replaying in my head. Then something dawned on me. How often has God had similar experiences with us? Are we afraid to even hope that he really wants us to enjoy all things, as if we should be happy with just spiritual-sounding activities? In my journey of discovering a radically normal faith, I've often thought, "Glorifying God couldn't possibly be this much fun." And yet the Bible says it can be.

This book is an invitation to joy—to find your eternal joy and satisfaction in God himself and then to delight in all the good gifts he gives. Do you lean toward being obsessively spiritual, undervaluing your everyday things? Or are you sometimes complacent, underestimating the importance of focusing your attention on God? Do you ever feel guilty for not being spiritual enough, or are you more likely to shove God to the corner of your life? Either way, I pray that God will use the following chapters to rescue you from the complacent and obsessive extremes.

Grace isn't just my oldest daughter's name; it's also the central thread holding this entire book together. Without a good grasp on grace, we could easily use it to excuse complacency or to find new ways to be obsessive. So let's talk about grace next.

2

Grasping Grace

How does a pastor lose 25 percent of his congregation? It's surprisingly easy. For instance, he can start using wine for communion without adequately preparing the congregation. That is sure to lose a family or two. For the record, I had the elders' full support and continued to offer grape juice as well. But I failed to realize how emotionally charged the change would be.

Foolish mistakes like that weren't the biggest problems, however. I'm a lousy administrator and don't have a good mind for details. Unfortunately, ignoring the business side of the church doesn't make it go away. Early in 2011 I began having a vague sense that the church budget was in rough shape. As the year continued, I realized that my faith and optimism were actually naïveté. On April 30, all the illusions came crashing down when the deacons told me the church had used up all its savings and I had to take desperate measures, including finding a second job.

Three weeks later, I found myself in the back room of the Mount Vernon Starbucks, putting on my green apron for the first time. I clearly remember the anxiety I felt. I was worried how my second job would affect my church. I also experienced the normal fears of a first day at work. Will I be able to keep up? Is this a big mistake? Will the other kids like me?

My biggest concern was how this would affect my family. Grace and Sarah thought my new job was cool, but I knew their enthusiasm would wear off as they started to feel my increased absence. I had to work closing shifts, which meant that three or four nights a week, Marilyn put them to bed without me. You have to understand that tucking my daughters into bed is still one of the best parts of my day. I seldom miss it and feel guilty when I do, as if I've lost something I can never regain. Even now, a year later, writing about those lost nights is difficult for me.

On the other hand, I was also a little excited. I'd always thought working at Starbucks would be fun. I love people, I love coffee, and Starbucks is a great place for both. I was also looking forward to a job that ended when I clocked off. The busyness of that job was a welcome distraction from church budgets, unfinished sermons, and other challenges of ministry.

I was also feeling other things that day—disappointment, doubt, and failure. This was not the story I had written in my head. I had a different picture of success and thought it would come more naturally. I hadn't planned on having to become a bivocational pastor. In theory, I believed working a second job in order to stay in ministry was a noble thing. In theory. But there I was, the second-oldest partner (employee) in the store, getting ready to serve coffee to the pastors I used to meet in that same Starbucks for coffee.

Coffee Ministry

The Starbucks era (as I now call it) wasn't the first time God has used coffee to help me grow. When my home church invited me to join the staff a decade earlier, it wasn't to fill a position, but because the senior pastor, Bruce, saw potential in me. I was pretty proud of that fact. But shortly after I started, we lost our receptionist, so guess what the brand-new, top-of-his-class pastor got to do? There I was, the most educated person on staff, answering phones and making coffee.

I wish I could say I humbly and gratefully accepted the post, but the truth is I resented it. I begrudged not being able to use my talents.

I was frustrated no one cared that I could read Greek and that Bruce discouraged the congregation from calling him (and me) Pastor. Making the coffee became the symbol of everything I resented. Every morning, I put it off as long as possible, hoping someone else would do it. When I actually did make the coffee, I wasn't terribly concerned about quality (no small offense in the Northwest) and wasn't very diligent to keep the coffee area clean.

I've since learned that we tend to turn our noses up at some of God's best gifts. We're like a young child who's just been given a $10,000 savings bond but would gladly trade it for a candy bar. Over the next few years, God used that coffee to confront my self-importance and teach me how to enjoy serving others. I began to see making the coffee as a gift—I carefully measured the coffee grounds and kept the area spotless. I started to pray for everyone who would drink the coffee that day. When we hired a receptionist, I actually missed making the coffee and even tried to arrive a little early each morning to make the first pot.

> We're like a young child who's just been given a $10,000 savings bond but would gladly trade it for a candy bar.

So you'd think I would have welcomed my job at Starbucks as a new learning opportunity. Instead, my feelings were mixed at best. I begged God to make everything go back to how it used to be, and I found myself resenting Starbucks just as I had resented being a receptionist. But I also knew that God was still very much in control and that he didn't do anything randomly. Sitting in the back room of Starbucks, reading the company's sexual harassment policy, I reluctantly believed my time there would be a gift, which is to say, an act of grace.

Running the Race

Many Christians think that grace basically means "Jesus saved me from my sins and now I get to go to heaven." But grace is far bigger than that.

A couple years ago, I ran my first half-marathon. It was actually fun in a "that didn't suck as much as I thought it would" sort of way. It was a cool and clear January morning, a perfect day for a race. We ran through the Skagit farmland, past fields, barns, and cows, with bald eagles circling overhead (watching for stragglers, I suppose). The foothills were covered in snow and looked glorious in the rare winter sun. Between the view and the conversations with my friend, I almost didn't notice how much my feet hurt.

For this race, runners chose between running a 5k (3.1 miles), 10k (6.2 miles), or half-marathon (13.1 miles). At the end of the race, the 5k and 10k runners received a nice little finisher's ribbon. But the half-marathoners got a finisher's medal. A couple of miles into the race, the half-marathoners kept going straight while the 5k and 10k folks went to the right. I felt smug about running the "real" race. That smugness diminished significantly when I was passed by several senior ladies. It was completely gone two hours later when I crossed the finish line and narrowly avoided throwing up on the guy who handed me my medal.

Some Christians think grace means God paid your entry fees and put you on the race course, but now it's up to you to run the race. Other Christians think grace means that if you try really, really hard but complete only the 5k race, God will give you a marathoner's medal anyway because he's nice that way. Neither of those goes nearly far enough.

To run with the racing analogy, grace means you're a quadriplegic who can't afford a wheelchair, let alone the entry fee. Grace means that the only way you'll get on the racetrack is if Jesus pays your fee and carries you onto the course. Grace means that the only way you'll run the race is if Jesus carries you every step of the way. And grace means you'll cross the finish line and receive the finisher's crown solely because Jesus carried you across.

What's your role in all this? Your biggest job is letting Jesus carry you through the race. Invariably, this proves too much for you and me, and we end up head butting Jesus until he lets us wallow in the mud of our sin. Keep in mind that those are cow pastures you're running by, so that isn't actually mud. Eventually, we come to our senses and ask him to carry us again.

Dangerous Cliffs

If that's also true, is grace a convenient excuse to coast in complacency and do whatever we want? That question shows how little we understand grace. Grace saves us from both obsessive and complacent Christianity. It frees us from both legalism and sin.

Years ago, my friend Jason went hiking in the mountains of Tajikistan along the border of Afghanistan. Americans weren't particularly popular in that part of the world, so he admits it wasn't one of the brighter things he's done. He said the trip up the mountain was hard enough, but coming down was a nightmare. His party was thousands of feet above the valley, making its way down what could be called a path only in the most generous sense of the word. It ran along a narrow ridge and was covered with jagged, loose gravel. Because the decline was so steep on each side, he didn't actually walk down the path—he slid.

"The trickiest part was staying on the ridge with only a couple feet of leeway on either side," Jason said. "If you focused too much on the dangers of one side, you naturally overcompensated and started to slide down the other side. The whole way down we had to constantly adjust our slide to avoid going too far off either side to a rather painful end."

Jason survived and went on to get married, have kids, and take up safer activities, including raising poison dart frogs (he assures me they lose their poison in captivity) and being a missionary in Bolivia.

Picture yourself on that same path, but make it narrower and the drop-off steeper than whatever you imagined. Add fierce winds howling around you, nearly pushing you off one side and then the other. Now imagine a rope anchored every 20 feet and running the entire length of the path. Only when you're grasping the rope do you dare to look up and enjoy the stunning view before you.

> Jesus had saved them from one cliff, and they were getting ready to cannonball off the other.

That path describes your Christian journey. The cliff to the left is destructive disobedience. This is complacent Christianity. The cliff to the right is legalism, trying to earn God's favor by doing all the right things and being a good person. This is obsessive Christianity. Fall off either cliff, and you'll end up in slavery.

The apostle Paul wrote, "It is for freedom that Christ has set us free. Stand firm, then, and do not let yourselves be burdened again by a yoke of slavery" (Galatians 5:1). He wrote "burdened again" because the Galatians had been saved from slavery to idols and sin, and now they were on the verge of being enslaved to legalism. Jesus had saved them from one cliff, and they were getting ready to cannonball off the other.

What does this have to do with grace? Grace is the rope that keeps you on the path. God's grace, secured by Christ's death, got us on the path in the first place. Grasping onto his grace is the only way we can stay on the path and enjoy the journey. And only by his grace can we safely make it home. No matter how many times we fall off the path, Jesus is ready to pull us back up by his grace.

Now I want you to imagine staying on that path without the rope. Does it sound difficult? Actually, it's not difficult—it's impossible. The winds of selfishness, lust, bitterness, and a host of other sinful desires threaten to blow us over the left cliff of destructive sin. As soon as we get control over those desires, we begin to feel pretty good about ourselves, and we're hit by winds of pride and self-righteousness, pushing us toward the right cliff of legalism. Our only hope, every step of the way, is desperate dependence on God's grace.

To be radically normal is to stay on the path and avoid both cliffs, completely dependent on grace.

The problem with the analogy is that it doesn't convey how joy-filled the journey is. Try to imagine experiencing some of your happiest moments while walking along that narrow path—seeing your newborn child, going to Disneyland, enjoying your favorite meal…

Now we're getting closer.

My time at Starbucks was a gift of grace. Through it, God helped me experience things I had only known in theory. For instance, God was kind enough to teach me a lot about patience through difficult customers. None of them tested my patience more than one particularly exuberant Christian. I'll introduce her to you in the next chapter.

It's Okay to Be Normal

At first, I was nervous about being "on bar" at Starbucks—making the drinks. I had to memorize a thick book of recipes and was expected to make all of them quickly and accurately. One night after work, I had a nightmare that I was in Disneyland making complicated espresso drinks for the White Witch. That was weird.

I also had to learn how to "call" drinks properly. That's how partners are able to keep up with all the customers' strange drink variations. Have you ever thought baristas were being snobby by correcting how you order drinks? They were actually using a system that allows them to remember your order more easily. So even though "personal decaf triple tall vanilla with room Americano" may sound like a barrage of information to you, the wording makes your order manageable for them.

My fears about being able to keep up were unfounded. Turns out I was pretty good on bar. In fact, it was my favorite position at the store—except when Iced Tea Lady came in.

Iced Tea Lady stood a head taller than most people and had a loud raspy voice that could be heard from across the store. She always ordered the cheapest drink on the menu, never tipped, and wanted us to think up a new variation each time. She thought we liked the challenge. In reality, most of us found it annoying. But that was not the worst part. What really bothered me was that Iced Tea Lady was a Christian. Not a quiet, polite Christian, but a loud, "Praise the Lord!" Christian who insisted on calling me "Pastor Josh." On one occasion, I made her yet another variation of iced tea and handed it to her, saying (with far more enthusiasm than I felt), "I hope you like it!" She loudly responded, "Don't worry, Jesus always makes it taste good!" (I wish I were making this up.) I politely excused myself, went to the back room, and banged my head against the freezer door.

I like to think of myself as a reasonably patient person, but I've discovered that I have a low tolerance for super-spiritual Christians. That's because I used to be one.

The Bad Thing About Being a Good Kid

Many Christian books start out with a call to be radical, which is largely a good thing. I'm starting with a call to be normal because that has been a bigger struggle for me. I grew up in a loving, conservative Christian home. When I was about 12 years old, I started to take my faith seriously. At an age when many of my peers started rebelling, I got closer to God. I wasn't trying to please my parents; it was genuinely what I wanted. In sixth grade, I refused to look at a friend's *Playboy* magazine. I didn't say bad words—I remember the shame I felt the first time I accidently said "What the hell?" I never smoked or drank, and to this day I don't really know what marijuana smells like.

Really, I don't. Just last week I was on a Greyhound bus returning from a writers' conference, and apparently someone started smoking a joint on board. The driver came on the intercom and said, "Come on, guys! 'No smoking' means 'no pot.' We can all smell it. Show some respect." The rest of the passengers chuckled, but I was disappointed that I hadn't been paying enough attention and still didn't know what pot smelled like.

Naive as I might be about the ways of the world, I still don't regret any of those decisions—they've saved me from a world of heartache. I might not have all the war stories of a rebellious youth, but neither do I have the battle wounds on my soul. But looking back, I wish I hadn't fallen prey to the spiritual pride that came with being a good little Christian. I was better at it than any of my peers, and I knew it. While many of my friends were sliding toward the cliff of destructive sins, I was sliding toward the cliff of self-righteousness.

As a teenager, I mentally created a two-tiered Christianity. At the bottom were the normal Christians and at the top were the super-Christians. I had the ugly habit of categorizing everyone. Did you listen to secular music? Normal Christian. Did you speak in tongues? Super-Christian. Did you sleep with your girlfriend? You probably weren't saved. My greatest fear as a teenager wasn't being uncool—it was being a normal Christian.

The super-Christian mentality was common in youth groups, especially in Pentecostal churches. We sang songs like "Sold Out and Radical" and went to conferences with names like "Only the Committed." My youth group days were valuable to my spiritual growth, but these things inadvertently reinforced a two-tiered Christianity. The call to be a super-Christian appealed to my pride at being better than normal Christians.

Radical Randy

Early in my pursuit of super-Christianity, I spent some of my paper route money on a Christian book for young teens. I discovered I should find a mentor, which I interpreted to mean I should find an older Christian who could show me how to be a super-Christian. The teenage years being what they are, I didn't even consider my own parents. I thought about a couple of other candidates, but they just didn't seem to be spiritual enough.

Then I met Radical Randy. He was barely five feet tall, but what he lacked in stature, he made up with volume. His crew-cut dishwater-blond hair gave him the look of a drill sergeant. He wore a cross the size of a small cat and had a large, submissive family. He was my first example of an obsessive Christian. My lasting impression is not of a man deeply in love with Jesus but of someone whose very strict version of Christianity dominated every square inch of his life.

Radical Randy taught me that the closer you were to Jesus, the less normally you talked. Even "How are you?" was answered, "Blessed, brother!" If being worldly means trying to fit in, Randy wasn't worldly at all. He acted as if he lived on another planet and visited this one as infrequently as possible. He was like John the Baptist in an outdated three-piece suit.

Radical Randy was also a street preacher. In my mind, that made him more spiritual than a pastor, so I began hanging out with him in order to study how to be a super-Christian. But as each outreach approached, I felt a growing knot in my stomach. I was ashamed to admit it, but I hated street preaching. The stomach flu would have been a welcome reprieve. I figured something must be wrong with me. Was I merely a normal Christian after all?

Even as I tried to power through street ministry, something else made me even more miserable. I didn't know how to talk or behave in front of Randy. Having a conversation was like walking through a minefield. Anything I said or did might be condemned as too worldly— not wearing a cross, listening to rock music (even Christian rock), or using an NIV Bible. Many things that my parents thought were perfectly fine were not spiritual enough for Radical Randy. Part of me couldn't stand being with him, but the other part was sure I just wasn't spiritual enough.

I used to look forward to a lifetime of following Jesus, but now I began to dread it.

All this time, I had a growing fear that if I were going to be a super-Christian, I'd have to be as obsessive as Randy. How much longer until I had to burn my Christian tapes, use a King James Bible, and start speaking Christianese? I loved God and wanted to obey him, so I was willing to pay that price. But a dangerous and horrifying change was happening in me. I used to look forward to a lifetime of following Jesus, but now I began to dread it.

I can't remember how long my time with Randy lasted. It felt like a year, but in reality it couldn't have been more than a month or two. I just couldn't handle it anymore—the dreaded street preaching, the impossibly high standards of holiness, and above all, the fear of having to be an obsessive Christian. In true teenage fashion, I just ignored the whole thing and hoped it would disappear. I stopped hanging out with him and tried to fade away, which was a little awkward in a church of 150 people. He just let me go quietly—I think he was used to people not measuring up.

The Two-Tier Trap

After that, I began an unconscious quest to discover what whole-hearted devotion to God really looked like. This book is something of a record of that quest. Did devotion mean being obsessive, like Randy? Or could a fully devoted follower of Christ be more normal, like my parents? Their love for God was obvious and affected every part of their lives, but my dad worked in a lumber mill, and my mom was a home-maker. My dad even got a regular paycheck. Randy had to live on faith. Isn't it more spiritual to trust God for your rent?

Years later I discovered there was nothing new about my two-tiered Christianity. It's been around for centuries. In the bottom tier were all the ordinary or carnal Christians, and in the top were the priests and saints (in Roman Catholicism), sanctified Christians (in the holiness movement), or Spirit-filled Christians (in Pentecostalism).[1] It's kind of like a spiritual version of the haves and have-nots.

From personal experience, I already knew how damaging the two-tiered mentality was for those presumptuous enough to assign them-selves to the top. As a pastor, I've discovered how detrimental it is for those who believe they belong on the bottom tier. Most Christians look at the greats—the apostle Paul, Francis of Assisi, Mother Teresa—and decide they can never measure up. Or they look at missionaries, street preachers, and pastors and feel certain that they just aren't on the same level as professional Christians. Too many Christians feel guilty for their normal, everyday lives, which doesn't involve performing mira-cles, standing behind a pulpit, or sharing the gospel in a distant jungle.

I've come to believe that the entire system is absolute nonsense, a trap of the enemy that puffs up a few Christians and deflates the rest. It immobilizes everyone who buys into it. Here's how I came to that conclusion.

Testing the Tiers

Whatever happened to Radical Randy? My family moved away, so I didn't hear much about him except that he had left our church because of a doctrinal issue. Later, I heard a rumor that he had an affair and deserted his family. As awful as it sounds, my first reaction was relief. I felt bad for his family, but this was the first hint of something I desperately hoped to be true—being an authentically godly person doesn't necessarily mean being obsessive.

I wanted to believe that being a fully devoted follower of Christ didn't require being obsessive and totally disconnected from this world. At the same time, I was suspicious of that desire. Was I just trying to water down the gospel? On one hand, the Bible was filled with prophets and apostles who looked uncomfortably like Radical Randy. I couldn't deny that God called some of his servants to be very strange—even telling Ezekiel to cook his dinners over human excrement. (Much to Ezekiel's relief, God compromised and let him use cow manure instead.)

On the other hand, the obsessive Christians I knew personally were seldom filled with love, joy, peace, or any other fruit of the Spirit (Galatians 5:21-23). They were judgmental, self-important, angry, and miserable. Conversely, the Christians I admired for their spiritual fruit were surprisingly normal. Something wasn't adding up. Either the Bible was encouraging me to be the sort of person I naturally avoided or else I misunderstood what the Bible was saying. I needed to know if the radical lifestyle of the biblical prophets and apostles was the gold standard we were supposed to strive for.

In Bible college I learned how to find my answers by reading the Bible more carefully. Context is king, we were told. Never just read one verse, our professors said, always look at the context. Not just the context of the surrounding verses, but the cultural and historical context of each book. The Bible was not written in a vacuum, but by real people to real people in real circumstances. If we ignore the cultural and historical context, we will likely miss the entire point.

Look at it this way. In the off chance you own an actual telephone book, take a look at the first several pages. You'll find a section about what to do after a major disaster—turn off your natural gas, use the water in your hot water tank for drinking, keep your fridge closed as much as possible, and listen to a battery-operated radio for instructions. These are great suggestions for times of emergency. But if you were to apply these instructions to everyday life, you'd be hunkered down in your house, huddled around an AM radio and eating cold Spam while your neighbors were outside enjoying a barbecue.

God called the prophets to do some pretty weird things because that's what their situations called for.

With that in mind, look at the context of these saints. Ezekiel walked around naked in a time of national crisis in order to shock a complacent nation. John the Baptist munched on crickets dipped in honey while ushering in the turning point of human history. Several books of the Bible were written in times of political and spiritual emergencies, and we must be careful how we apply them to our lives. In what ways does our situation match theirs, and in what ways is it different?

Here's the point. God called the prophets to do some pretty weird things because that's what their situations called for. Their stories continue to encourage and inspire us, but they don't necessarily provide point-by-point direction on how to live in our contemporary situations. When we focus on only a few figures with unique missions in extreme times, we miss just how much the Bible has to say to the majority of believers who are trying to live normal lives in ordinary circumstances.

Granted, many Christians don't think we are living in ordinary circumstances. Time and time again we're told these are the last days. I grew up believing that the Soviet Union was the great beast of Revelation. When I was in the eighth grade, one of the bestselling Christian books was *88 Reasons Why the Rapture Will Be in 1988*. The followup book, *The Final Shout: Rapture Report 1989* didn't sell quite as well Going further back, some Christians in my grandfather's generation didn't keep a savings account because they were sure Jesus would return before they'd need it. Even further back, the apostle Paul had to address end-time mania in 1 and 2 Thessalonians. After two millennia of false alarms, all the end-time drama starts to ring hollow. Yes, Jesus is coming back, and we must be ready, but it might be a while, so we must be ready for that too.

Once I understood that the Bible wasn't just written to people in crisis situations, I began to see God's interest in normal life hidden in plain sight.

The Bible and Normal Life

I recently finished a three-year series preaching through the Bible. For me, the biggest surprise of the series was discovering how much I enjoyed the Torah and the Mosaic Law.[2] In it, I was able to see God's interest in everyday life. Chapter after chapter deals with normal, earthly things—from crop rotation to another very practical matter: "As part of your equipment have something to dig with, and when you relieve yourself, dig a hole and cover up your excrement" (Deuteronomy 23:13).

Are you surprised that verse is in the Bible? It seems so unspiritual. By the way, did you know that Jesus talked about using a toilet? See if you can spot it: "'Are you still so dull?' Jesus asked them. 'Don't you see that whatever enters the mouth goes into the stomach and then out of the body?'" (Matthew 15:16-17).

Did you find it? No? That's because almost all English translations leave it out. The Greek actually says, "Whatever enters the mouth goes into the stomach and is expelled into the toilet." I wonder why translators felt the need to censor that out? What does that say about how we read the Bible? I'll tell you one thing, God is far more comfortable discussing our bodily functions than we are. He doesn't blush when talking about menstrual cycles and nocturnal emissions. He is completely comfortable with the normal things of this life.

That alone doesn't prove that God is just as pleased by our normal lifestyles as he is the radical lifestyles of the prophets and apostles. One more point needs to be made. God ordained a small number of Israelites to be Levites, priests, and prophets. Yet he never treated them as super-Jews and the rest as just normal Jews. The priest and Levites had special jobs, but the Bible gives no hint that they were more obedient to God than the rest. God's intent was for all Israel to be "a kingdom of priests and a holy nation" (Exodus 19:6). Priests, prophets, farmers, shepherds, and carpenters all had equal opportunity to obey and serve God wholeheartedly, right where they were.

Once I saw that truth in the Old Testament, I began to see it in the New Testament as well. Jesus had 12 disciples, and there were only 120 followers in the upper room on Pentecost, but many more believed in him without leaving their daily lives.[3] The Samaritan believers stayed faithful in Sychar. Jesus told the man freed from demons to go back home instead of following him, and Mary's and Martha's normal lives provided Jesus with a place to stay.[4] Yes, some were called to radically alter their lifestyles by leaving everything and following Jesus, but most were equally obedient and commendable by staying home and following him from there.

This same pattern continues on a larger scale in the early church. A few were called to become missionaries, but the vast majority of Christians kept working the same jobs and living in the same houses. "Each one should live as a believer in whatever situation the Lord has assigned to them, just as God has them. This is the rule I lay down in all the churches" (1 Corinthians 7:17).

Where in the New Testament do we see the apostles telling early Christians to literally abandon everything for the sake of the gospel? Nowhere. Far from simply tolerating their normal lives, the apostles taught them how to be faithful in them. C.S. Lewis came to the same realization.

> Before I became a Christian I do not think I fully realized
> that one's life, after conversion, would inevitably consist in
> doing most of the same things one had been doing before,
> one hopes, in a new spirit, but still the same things.[5]

Happy to Be Normal

Somewhere along the way, I completely discarded my two-tiered Christianity and my super-Christian identity. I finally realized that I'm not any higher or lower than other followers of Jesus. I'm proud to live my normal life as a Christian, serving God alongside students, factory workers, retirees, and many others. Certainly, some Christians are more obedient than others. Some are sliding toward complacency and destructive sins. Others are sliding toward obsession and self-righteousness. But there's only one faith and one family.

Are You a Top-Tier Christian?

Are you desperate to believe that you're a better Christian than others? Would you feel crushed if you discovered that you were lumped in with all the regular Christians who don't try as hard as you? Of course, you'd never say that out loud because you know how arrogant it sounds. Is your identity determined less by being loved and accepted by Jesus and more by being a really good Christian? Is it hard for you to relax because you're working so hard to stay more spiritual than the masses?

I've been there. One time, when I was playing capture the flag with a group of missionaries, I lost my temper and kicked a guy where I ought not have. I was devastated, not because I really hurt him, but because I failed so publicly. I don't ever want to go back to being crushed by every little mistake. It feels amazing to be able to fail, repent, and not care what others think. Paul wrote about this to people like us.

> If anyone thinks they are something when they are not, they deceive themselves. Each one should test their own actions. Then they can take pride in themselves alone, without comparing themselves to someone else, for each one should carry their own load (Galatians 6:3-5).

Stop the comparisons. Repent of arrogance and self-sufficiency. Learn to rest and fall into Jesus's arms. Learn to fall into the arms of your Christian community. It's amazing how much I learned from other Christians once I stopped thinking I was better than them.

Are You a Bottom-Tier Christian?

Do you feel as if you're in the stands, watching all the major-league Christians down on the field? Are you convinced that God must be a little happier with super-Christians than he is with you? In theory, you know that you could join them on the field, but that would require changing everything and leaving behind everything you've ever known.

What mediocrity have you excused because you're "just" a normal Christian?

Here's what I'd say to you. You are not a sub-par Christian. You are not condemned to be a spectator. God is happy with you right where you are. You can be a fully obedient, devoted follower of Christ in the life God has given you.

By God's grace, you are the lead actor in your story, a story that he wrote for you and no one else. He chose your time in history, your family, your nationality, your skills, and your IQ. He wants to work through your experiences, your failures, your strengths, and your weaknesses. He can do things through you, right where you are, that he cannot do through anyone else. God isn't waiting for you to move to India to start working through you; he's just waiting for you to rely on his grace.

God gives us the same promise he gave regular Jews.

> But you [not just your pastor or the missionaries or the heroes of the faith, but *you*] are a chosen people, a royal priesthood, a holy nation, God's special possession, that you may declare the praises of him who called you out of darkness into his wonderful light (1 Peter 2:9, quoting Exodus 19:6).

That is good news. We can be free from the guilt of not measuring up. It can also be scary. It removes many of the excuses we might use to justify our lack of obedience. What complacency, what laziness, what mediocrity have you excused because you're "just" a normal Christian?

- I have house payments, so I can't serve God.
- I have kids, so I can't help out at the food bank.
- I don't have formal Bible education, so I can't share the gospel with my neighbor.
- I'm not a pastor, so I can't live up to all of God's standards.

The only thing standing between you and a life of wholehearted obedience isn't your job, place of birth, income, or knowledge of the Bible. It's your willingness to fall into Jesus's arms and lean completely on his grace. Repent of self-sufficiency—it was never about you or what you brought to the table anyway. It has always been about what God can do through people just like you and me.

Perhaps you think this is easy for me to say because I'm a pastor. I don't know what it's like to have a job that feels meaningless or to struggle with feelings of spiritual inadequacy. You might have been right until I started working at Starbucks. That was where God taught me the value of hard work and showed me just how inflated my view of vocational ministry really was.

4

Honorable Work

I seldom introduce myself as Pastor Josh anymore because most people act differently in front of a pastor. Besides, it's hilarious to watch them panic when they do find out. Now that I'm over my obsession with being a top-tier Christian, I'm sensitive to the perception that pastors are somehow different from or better than anyone else. Even before I worked at Starbucks, I'd remind my church that they don't have to be in full-time ministry to please God and that they can honor him equally well in their current jobs. I said it so often, I thought I believed it.

But as soon as I started working at Starbucks, I began struggling to find meaning in my job. What's the spiritual significance of making four-dollar lattes? Did cleaning the lobby really matter in light of eternity? I occasionally got to do things that sounded more spiritual, like having meaningful conversations with fellow partners, but those were the exception. If the value of my work was judged by the number of people I ministered to in traditional ways, I was failing. If it was judged by the number of people I converted to Christianity, I failed completely.

Life became routine. Every Monday through Thursday, I'd head into my Starbucks well before my shift began, dressed in khaki pants and black polo shirt, with my green apron neatly rolled up in my computer bag. I'd sit in the lobby and work on my sermon all morning. In the afternoon, I'd lock my computer in my '92 Buick LeSabre with its peeling paint, clock in, and start selling coffee.

The best part of my day was after I got home. Every night, I'd slip upstairs to kiss my sleeping daughters goodnight (always a bittersweet moment), spend some time with Marilyn, and go back downstairs to work on this book. I loved my church, but I was pretty discouraged about our financial situation, and writing became my refuge. Whenever my mind wandered, it invariably found its way to a chapter or concept I was working on.

One evening, when I was sweeping the lobby, I finally hit a breaking point. As I swept, I was thinking some really deep thoughts about the Old Testament and how it applies to everyday life. Suddenly, my job at Starbucks felt so meaningless. I'd swept this same floor a hundred times before and would sweep it again the next day. Nearly in tears, I begged God to let me quit this pointless job and go back to my real calling.

It's not often that I say "the Holy Spirit told me" because I've heard that statement followed by some pretty goofy stuff. But in one instant, he showed me my hypocrisy. The same deep thought I had just been thinking now condemned my bad attitude. But it also freed me from a burden I had been carrying for 20 years. I'll get back to that deep thought shortly, but first let me tell you about the burden.

Called to Go?

I was 15 when I first heard a call to the mission field. Not a call from God, mind you, but from Keith Green. Keith was a Christian musician whose popularity and influence extended well beyond his untimely death in 1982. *No Compromise* was not only the name of one of his albums, it was his philosophy. Keith was passionate about Jesus and reaching the lost. He was a radical figure who inspired a generation in powerful ways. But I believe that in his youthful zeal (he was only 28 when he died and had been a Christian for about seven years) he sometimes went too far.

My family owned a video of one of his concerts, which we watched often and even subjected our guests to. About halfway through the concert, Keith quoted from the Great Commission.

> Then Jesus came to them and said, "All authority in heaven and on earth has been given to me. Therefore go and make disciples of all nations, baptizing them in the name of the Father and of the Son and of the Holy Spirit, and teaching them to obey everything I have commanded you. And surely I am with you always, to the very end of the age" (Matthew 28:18-20).

Keith continued by saying that being a banker or lawyer for Jesus wasn't enough. "If you are not called to stay [in America], you are called to go," he said. "You don't need a call—you are already called. Unless you have received a definite call to stay, then you are called to go!" I can't convey on paper how convincing he was—listening to it again yesterday, I felt guilty for only being a pastor!

Keith's appeal inspired many men and women to become missionaries, but it also made many feel guilty. At the age of 15, I was being told that if I didn't become a missionary, I was rebelling against Jesus. I could support missionaries, pray for the lost, and serve Jesus in my community, but I'd still fall short. The problem was that I really didn't want to be a missionary (or a pastor, for that matter). Whenever I talked to God in my quiet times, I was careful not to listen too closely because I was afraid he would tell me to be a missionary. About five years later I realized that I might actually want to be a pastor, so I headed off to Bible college.

A High Calling

At Bible college, the emphasis on being in vocational ministry continued. I can't count the number of times I heard that being in full-time ministry was a high calling. The professors and chapel speakers frequently reminded us just how few students would enter full-time ministry and that even fewer would survive their first five years. I know they meant well—they were trying to inspire us and prepare us for the trials ahead. But their warnings included a subtle challenge: "Will *you* be one of the few to make it?" The problem with telling a bunch of young, self-confident students that the ministry is a noble profession is that they start to believe it's the only noble profession. The challenge reinforced the fallacy of a two-tiered Christianity.

I wonder how many of my classmates still feel as if they failed God because they didn't remain in vocational ministry.

What spoke the loudest wasn't what was said, but what wasn't said. I don't ever remember a chapel speaker saying, "Seventy-five percent of you won't graduate from here—and that's great! We're excited for whatever God has for you. Take everything you learn here and use it wherever you go. God knows this world could use more biblically trained business leaders, interior designers, and computer programmers."(Thankfully, this has changed. My alma mater now speaks with pride about its bivocational alumni and offers programs for students who plan work outside of the church.)

I wonder how many of my classmates still feel as if they failed God because they didn't remain in vocational ministry. I talked to one Bible-college dropout who told me this supposed failure was a factor in his broken marriage. It wasn't the only factor to be sure, but his ex-wife made it clear that she wanted to be married to a pastor, not a used-car salesman. Likewise, I wonder how many former missionaries and pastors struggle to find meaning and God's approval in their post-ministry lives.

I've also talked to many Christians who believe they're second-class Christians because they're not in vocational ministry. They live under the burden of believing that God would have been a little happier if they had sold everything and become missionaries.

Almost as Good

For the past 20 years, I'd been afraid that Keith Green was at least partially right. In light of eternity, what business do any of us have doing anything other than preaching the gospel? On the surface, that sentiment seemed so biblical, and I had never heard a pastor refute it. The basic response was more pragmatic. If everybody went on the mission field, who would support the missionaries? God's plan for supporting missions seemed to be based on the majority of us being disobedient.

"But that's okay," the church seemed to say. "We don't want you to feel too bad—you can make up for it by going to church, paying your tithe, supporting our missionaries, teaching Sunday school, and being a good witness at work. Winning coworkers to Jesus is almost as good as being a missionary." These things were consolation prizes for not being in vocational ministry. But what if you hate teaching Sunday school? What if you work all by yourself, and the only one you could witness to is the squirrel watching you dig a ditch? Of course, no one would actually say any of that, but the problem was what Christian leaders *didn't* say. I heard lots of sermons about supporting missions and being a good witness at work, but I don't remember many sermons about honoring God through hard work.

But I was set free that evening in Starbucks. I realized my job had meaning—and not only because I was fulfilling the Great Commission by witnessing or tithing. It had meaning because it was fulfilling another commission that preceded the other by several millennia. Before I explain that, I need to tell you about the deep thought I had been thinking as I swept the floor that night.

The Bible Jesus Read

I would be exaggerating if I said Christians never read the Old Testament, but not by much. We know the Sunday school stories, the Ten Commandments, parts of Psalms and Proverbs, and a smattering of the messianic prophecies. But many Christians treat the Old Testament the way they do the preface in other books—they know it might be important, but they skip it anyway.

The authors of the New Testament didn't see it that way. What we call the Old Testament, they called the Bible. They quoted the Old

Testament continually, viewed it as authoritative, and lived their lives by its precepts. Far from treating the Old Testament as the preface to the Bible, they saw it as the core. They wrote Gospels and history and letters and such to explain the staggering ramification of Jesus's life, death, resurrection, and ascension. They didn't write to replace the Old Testament, but to supplement it.

Here's why this is so important. The authors of the New Testament had no intention of replacing the Old Testament, so they could be selective about what they wrote. They didn't need to cover every single topic, because they expected their readers to know the Old Testament. For example, the New Testament doesn't talk a lot about worship because we have Psalms to teach us how to worship God.

Here's another example. The New Testament doesn't say much about sex beyond "don't do it outside of marriage."[1] If all we had was the New Testament, we might think God had a low view of sex. If you want to see just how pro-sex the Bible really is, read Proverbs and the Song of Solomon—an entire book dedicated to unabashed sexual enjoyment.

> Much of what I call obsessive Christianity is the result of reading only the New Testament at the expense of the Old.

The more I study the Bible, the more I realize that the apostles expected their readers to continue receiving instruction from the Old Testament. When we don't read the Old Testament enough, we get an incomplete picture of what God is telling us. Much of what I call obsessive Christianity is the result of reading only the New Testament at the expense of the Old. That's kind of funny when you think about it. Like most Christians, I used to associate the Old Testament with wrath and rules and no fun. In reality, the Old Testament is packed with parties and feasts and lots of fun.

The First Great Commission

As I was thinking about how the Old and New Testaments work together to give us the whole picture of the Christian life, I suddenly realized something I had never seen before. The Great Commission at the end of Matthew was not the first Great Commission. Jesus gave it to us assuming that we would keep following the first one, which is found at the very beginning of the Bible.

> Then God said, "Let us make mankind in our image, in our likeness, so that they may rule over the fish in the sea and the birds in the sky, over the livestock and all the wild animals, and over all the creatures that move along the ground."
>
> So God created mankind in his own image,
>   in the image of God he created them;
>   male and female he created them.
>
> God blessed them and said to them, "Be fruitful and increase in number; fill the earth and subdue it. Rule over the fish in the sea and the birds in the sky and over every living creature that moves on the ground" (Genesis 1:26-28).

The first Great Commission, God's very first command to humanity, was to work in the garden, take care of it, and rule over the earth. We were made in his image, which means (among other things) that we are to be his representatives to the entire earth. "Fill the earth and subdue it" doesn't mean "trash it as quick as you possibly can," but "take good care of it on God's behalf." God told Adam not only to rule but also to work. "The Lord God took the man and put him in the Garden of Eden to work it and take care of it" (Genesis 2:15).

Before sin entered the world, God's plan for his children was that they work hard and enjoy the fruits of their labor. Work—hard, sweaty, and down-in-the-dirt work—was a big part of his original plan for us.

When you swing a hammer, teach kids, network computers, or drive a bus, you are fulfilling the first Great Commission.

Adam's sin and the events of Genesis 3 didn't negate the first Great Commission, but only necessitated the addition of the second Great Commission of Matthew 28. A God-honoring, radically normal life isn't obsessed with the second Great Commission to the exclusion of the first one. Nor does it complacently acknowledge the first while ignoring the second.

Keith Green was speaking biblically when he said Jesus commands us all to go, but he wasn't speaking biblically enough. He overlooked the first Great Commission as well as the practice of the early church. Paul never told his readers to quit their jobs and go onto the mission field. Rather, he told the majority of them to stay put.

That evening in the Starbucks lobby, I finally understood that our hard work honors God. Giving a tithe of our earnings or preaching to coworkers doesn't make it holier. Just by making the four-dollar lattes with excellence and sweeping the floor the best I could, I was honoring God. I was fulfilling the first Great Commission.

Think how radically this could change your view of work—when you swing a hammer, teach kids, network computers, or drive a bus, you are fulfilling the first Great Commission. Unless you are convinced that God has called you into vocational ministry, stop worrying about it. You can just focus on working hard and glorifying God in whatever job you may find yourself. (Well, maybe not whatever job—I seriously doubt you could be a pimp to the glory of God.)[2]

So God doesn't expect us all to become missionaries. Does that mean that we should be content with mediocre lives and never strive to great things in the kingdom of God? No, mediocrity is the last thing God wants for you or me. God wants us to be great. He wants your corner of the world to be different because you are there. The thing is, we tend to have a distorted view of greatness. Let's talk about that next.

5

Greatness for Average Joes

The weekly task of writing a sermon is the best and worst part of a pastor's job. I once heard a pastor say it's like having a baby on Sunday and discovering on Monday that you're pregnant again. One of the biggest challenges I faced as a bivocational pastor was finding enough time to write my sermons. In order to kill two birds with one stone, I decided to preach through some of the topics of this book.

My first sermon in the series was roughly based on chapter 3, "It's Okay to Be Normal." I could tell that most of the church was enjoying the message, but Nate sat in his third-row seat furrowing his eyebrows. After church he and I had a little conversation. "If my wife and I would have followed your advice about being normal," he said, "we would never have adopted Odessa." I had to agree, adopting a child from India who might have special needs isn't exactly what most people would call normal.

Is that what I wanted? To discourage Christians from doing great, radical things? If I had preached my sermon a year earlier, would Odessa still be stuck in an orphanage? Can radically normal Christians be radically obedient without being obsessive? What if Mother Teresa had been satisfied with the status quo? Or what if the apostle Paul had been content just making tents?

I knew that wasn't what I meant—I wanted to see a church filled with believers pursuing greatness, not mediocrity. What was the difference between Nate's radical sacrifice and obsessive Christianity?

The Body of Christ

I'll tell you in a minute how I responded to Nate's objection. First, think about the expression "the body of Christ." We use it so frequently that we forget it isn't so much a title of the church as an illustration.

> Just as a body, though one, has many parts, but all its many parts form one body, so it is with Christ. For we were all baptized by one Spirit so as to form one body—whether Jews or Gentiles, slave or free—and we were all given the one Spirit to drink. Even so the body is not made up of one part but of many (1 Corinthians 12:12-14).

The church is like your body, made up of many different parts, each with a special job. You may not think about how important fingernails are until you cut one way too short and discover how much your fingertips need to be protected. Each part of the body of Christ has a vital role to play, yet most parts either overvalue or undervalue their role.

The beauty of Paul's analogy is that it so effectively illustrates how much each part needs the others. A couple years ago, I needed to build a fence around our backyard, but I'm an abysmal handyman. Assembling IKEA furniture pushes the limits of my building skills. Fortunately, I have a lot of friends who are good at building. They helped me build the fence—mostly by keeping me out of the way with simple jobs while they built the fence. After watching me try to use a hammer for several minutes, one guy stepped in and asked, "You don't do this very often, do you?" I suppose I could have been insulted, but instead I just laughed. I love the way God made me, with all my strengths and weaknesses, yet I'm keenly aware of how much I need the rest of the body.

> If the whole body were an eye, where would the sense of hearing be? If the whole body were an ear, where would the sense of smell be? But in fact God has placed the parts in

the body, every one of them, just as he wanted them to be. If they were all one part, where would the body be? As it is, there are many parts, but one body (1 Corinthians 12:17-20).

Have you ever compared yourself to some other part of the body and come up short? Maybe you think, "I could never care for the poor like Mother Teresa." Or "My pastor is much better at comforting hurting people than I am." Of course you can't do what they do—you're not them. We have a habit of comparing ourselves at our weakest point to other people at their strongest. But don't forget that they have their weaknesses too.

My wife makes a far better mother than I ever will. I lack many of the necessary qualifications for that job, but that hardly makes me a failure. I make a better father than she does. Joy isn't found by being good at someone else's job, but by playing your part and allowing others to play theirs.

I think it's pretty clear no one gets to be the entire body, yet it's easy to create a composite picture in our heads of ideal Christians. They pray and read the Bible an hour a day and witness door-to-door. They are warm and outgoing and immensely gifted in ministry, yet they never struggle with pride. They're secure in God's love, yet they easily empathize with the hurting. They always know when to comfort and when to confront in love.

This is a myth. No such people exist, nor could they unless they lived off of a large inheritance and had multiple personalities. Our composites are made of contradictory skills and personalities. The man who excels at mercy usually struggles with confronting. The woman who has never doubted God's love doesn't naturally understand her friends who struggle day by day with acceptance. Our weaknesses aren't flaws in our design—they're features of it. The body needs each part in order to get the job done. God designed us to need not only his grace but also each other.

Different Calls
Your individual strengths and weaknesses give you a unique place

in the body of Christ. So do the specific roles and callings that you get excited about. Think of some of the many things God has called the church to do.

> speaking truth with boldness
>
> helping people
>
> teaching about God and the Bible
>
> encouraging the downtrodden
>
> providing for those in need
>
> leading others
>
> sharing grace and mercy

This list is based on Romans 12:6-8. As you read through it, I'll bet that some items excite you more than others. As I've said, no one person can do everything that needs to be done. God has made some of us passionate about certain things and some of us excited about others. Whenever we focus exclusively on one calling (as Keith Green seemed to do with missions) and try to tell all Christians they must pursue that one calling, we're implying the church doesn't need any eyes, just a whole bunch of mouths.

Here's an example of how I've learned to appreciate someone else's calling. Some pastors are Democrats, and some are Republicans. I'm just this side of apathetic. The biggest problem in my country isn't which political party is in power but how much sin is in people's hearts. Jesus is the only effective way to fix that problem, so I'd rather put my effort into changing hearts with the gospel.[1] It's fair to say that politics isn't my calling.

At one time, I used to think my calling as a pastor was higher than a calling to politics. Then I watched the movie *Amazing Grace* and had to acknowledge that God called William Wilberforce to help end slavery in the British Empire. Frankly, I don't want every Christian to adopt my attitude toward politics. Woe to us if Christians were to abandon the political arena. God has impassioned many Christians to make a lasting impact through politics, and I gladly encourage them.

Your High Calling

After Nate challenged me that Sunday morning about adopting Odessa, I spent most of the afternoon brooding and trying to understand the difference between radical obedience and obsessive obedience. Then it hit me, and I quickly called his cell phone. No answer. I couldn't wait, so I left this message.

"Nate, if I were to adopt a child from India because I thought that's what good Christians do, that would be obsessive. But you didn't adopt Odessa because someone said you should. Adopting her was what you really wanted to do. God had been preparing you to do this for years. It was a great sacrifice, a radical sacrifice, but it was also your joy."

Similarly, I'm not in vocational ministry because that's what obedient Christians do, but because I'm doing what I love. Preaching is not a higher or better calling than building a house, teaching preschool, or collecting trash. But it's my calling.

> I don't want you to go be a missionary or pastor unless you're sure God has called you to—not because it's too ambitious or too great for you, but because it's below you.

I don't want you to go be a missionary or pastor unless you're sure God has called you to—not because it's too ambitious or too great for you, but because it's below you. The highest calling you can find is the one God gave you. He made you, he knows how you tick, he knows your life stories and experiences, and he says, "Here's what you can do better than anyone else." Any other calling may sound noble, but it will be a distraction. Obsessive Christianity has distracted far too many believers from their real calling. If you've been told that you should be a missionary, it might be hard to see that your true calling is to be a really good barista with a listening ear.

The difference between being obsessive and being radically normal has nothing to do with the magnitude of your sacrifice or how strange it sounds to others. If your sacrifice is based on guilt, obligation, or legalism, you're being obsessive. However, if you do something because it's your joy to obey God in that way, you're being radically normal. I have some missionary friends who love what they're doing and really hope God doesn't call them back home. Yet they've known missionaries who are miserable and driven by obligation, not joy. Who do you think is more effective at sharing the love of God?

But what if you refuse to pursue your calling because it sounds too hard? What if all you want to do is play video games or be rich and go on lots of vacations? This is what I mean by nearsighted, complacent Christianity.

Low Ambitions

Our Starbucks had one customer who spent more hours at the store than I did. Moe was the stereotypical nerd. He dressed in outdated clothes that hung awkwardly on his skinny frame, and he wore thick glasses that had been out of style since…well, I doubt they had ever been in style. Each morning, Moe arrived at ten a.m. and stayed until around eight p.m. For almost ten hours, Moe would hide in the back corner and play video games. Other than asking for water or going to the bathroom, he'd just sit there, contentedly building and defending virtual kingdoms. Occasionally I'd envy his lack of responsibility (usually when I was banging my head against the wall trying to come up with a sermon), but most of the time I pitied him. His seemed to be an empty, depressing life.

We had other customers who worked hard, dressed nice, and tipped well. From the outside, they were on the opposite end of the spectrum from Moe. But as I watched them and overheard their conversations, I saw that their ambitions were just as low as Moe's. They were content to spend their time and energy building their own little kingdoms—being the big shots at work, having the hottest bodies at the gym, or making lots of money to spend on themselves. Their ambitions were as self-focused and shortsighted as playing video games all day.

That is not what God wants for you or me. He wants you to be great. He wants you to shine in this world "like stars in the sky as you hold firmly to the word of life."[2] He wants your life to count for something that outshines those stars. We are destined to advance the kingdom of God and change the world, to bring healing and hope to the earth and its inhabitants. Most of us aren't overly ambitious—we're not ambitious enough. We are, in the words of C.S. Lewis, too easily pleased.

How to Be Great

I recently read an inspiring book about editing your life and making it into something great. It was filled with inspirational stories of men and women who had charted their lives to some great purpose. I loved the way the author pushed me to intentionally craft each scene of my life. However, one thing about the book bothered me. Most of the stories were about people who already had something going for them at the outset, such as owning a multimillion-dollar business or being famous.

What about the rest of us? As I write this, I'm an unknown pastor whose greatest accomplishment has been shrinking his church from small to really small. I don't have the leadership ability to create a world-class nonprofit. Maybe you don't have the money to start a massive foundation the way Bill Gates has. Neither of us have been invited to serve as the chaplain for our favorite NFL team. Have you ever seen the poster that says "Potential" in big letters and has a picture of French fries? Under the picture is the caption, "Not everyone gets to be an astronaut when they grow up." Is that our fate? Do we simply lack the potential for greatness?

> Our problem with greatness isn't that we aren't capable of it, but that we have a distorted view of it.

My answer is a resounding no. I believe God destined all of his children to greatness. He doesn't have favorites. He didn't give the keys of the kingdom to a select few while the rest of us get safety scissors and crayons. Here's how I see it. If God's goal were efficiency, he probably wouldn't work through any of us. The least of his angels could probably do a better job than all of us combined.

I think of all the times I've had Grace and Sarah help me wash the car. Believe me, the point is not free labor. The job takes longer with their help, especially when Sarah gets hold of the hose. But that's okay because efficiency isn't my goal. I want to spend time with them while teaching them how to work. Likewise, I'm pretty sure that God's goal for working through us is to draw us closer to himself and to train us for eternity. The Bible hints that even now we're learning skills we'll need in heaven, where we will judge the angels.[3] Therefore, is greatness found by washing a bigger section of the car? Or does it have more to do with completing the tasks he has given us regardless of how insignificant they may seem?

Our propensity for idolizing celebrities shows that deep down we believe Christianity is about what humans can do, not what God does. Every one of us, from the apostle Paul to Billy Graham to you and me, desperately needs God's grace to accomplish anything. It is and has always been about him.

Our problem with greatness isn't that we aren't capable of it, but that we have a distorted view of it. The church unwittingly perpetuates this distortion by focusing more on celebrities than on everyday folks. Greatness isn't measured by the amount of money we give, the number of people we serve, or the books we write. Your greatness is measured by how completely you fulfill God's mission for you.

When you stand before your heavenly Father, he won't measure your greatness the same way we measure it on earth. He will measure by the way you responded to your calling. I've talked to people who've met famous actors, and they often say, "I thought he was taller," or "I thought she was prettier." I'm convinced that in heaven we'll be underwhelmed by the greatness of many of the celebrities of faith, not because they failed in some way, but because we had an inflated view of them. We will likely be surprised to find that many of the greats are men and women we have never heard of.

Finding Your Calling

So how do you find your calling, your path to greatness? What can you do better than Mother Teresa or Billy Graham? I was talking to my friend Heather about this because her calling (and career) is helping people find the perfect job to match their skills, passions, and experiences. Here are two questions she suggested to help you get started.

What Are You Good At?

Have you ever heard people say, "God equips the called rather than calling the equipped"? I cringe every time I hear that. I understand what they're trying to communicate—the greatest feats are done by men and women who feel so completely out of their depth that they have to desperately rely on God every step of the way. Amen. Yet God begins equipping you at the moment of conception—his empowerment is written in your DNA. Then he weaves together your strengths, weaknesses, and experiences to prepare you for your calling. Don't forget that by the time Paul was converted, God had spent years preparing him through his training under Gamaliel.[4] Likewise, Peter's passion and impetuousness (which caused him to lop off someone's ear one moment and deny Jesus the next) was molded, not overridden, by the Holy Spirit.[5]

What Do You Enjoy Doing?

My mom has had a passion for missions since I was young, but her greatest fear was that God would send her to India. That fear came from what I call "misery theology." I'm referring to the teaching that says, "Never say, 'God, please don't send me there' because that's where he will send you!" The idea is that if you refuse God in any area, that area becomes the most important battleground. That may be true enough, but misery theology implies that God is most happy when you're most miserable.

> "The place God calls you to is where your deep gladness and the world's deep hunger meet."
>
> —FREDERICK BUECHNER

My experience has been quite the opposite. If (and this is a big if) our desire is to obey God, he is more likely to lead us by the desires of our own hearts. After my siblings and I moved out of the house, my mom and dad were able to spend several years on the mission field. Where did God send them? Mexico. And they loved it.

Deep Gladness

I love the way author and pastor Frederick Buechner put it.

> The kind of work God usually calls you to is the kind of work (a) that you need most to do and (b) that the world most needs to have done. If you really get a kick out of your work, you've presumably met requirement (a), but if your work is writing cigarette ads, the chances are you've missed requirement (b). On the other hand, if your work is being a doctor in a leper colony, you have probably met requirement (b), but if most of the time you're bored and depressed by it, the chances are you have not only bypassed (a) but probably aren't helping your patients much either.
>
> Neither the hair shirt nor the soft berth will do. The place God calls you to is the place where your deep gladness and the world's deep hunger meet.[6]

My calling lies where my deep gladness to study and proclaim truth meets the world's need to know that truth. That's my calling. What's yours?

- Your deep gladness might be to care for the sick and dying, and the world's deep need is for nurses and caregivers filled with God's Spirit to bring his comfort into nursing homes and oncology wards.

- Your gladness might be to swing a hammer and build things (or tear them down!), and the world's need is for ethical carpenters who work hard, don't steal from their companies or clients, and are examples of God's love.

- Your gladness might be chatting with people and making coffee, and the world's need might be for caffeine made by people who genuinely care about their day and whisper a quick prayer under their breath.

- Your greatest passion might be to raise, nurture, and train children, and the world's need is for adults who have been loved, are well-disciplined, and follow Jesus.

If you could do anything for God and knew you couldn't fail, what would it be?[7] Don't focus on your shortcomings, but on his grace. I'm not promising that you'll accomplish that exact thing, but you're far more likely to find your true calling if you're moving in the right direction. Nor am I promising that you'll be able to make your living through your calling. Since my time at Starbucks, I've developed a great respect for people who work a full week and then pursue their calling in their free time.

I know the ambitions I have for my daughters. I want them to be great and excel at whatever they put their hands to. Part of the reason I have them help me wash the car is to prepare them for greatness. I'm convinced that my ambition for my children is a reflection of our heavenly Father's ambitions for us. "He who did not spare his own Son, but gave him up for us all—how will he not also, along with him, graciously give us all things?" (Romans 8:32).

If he loves and values you enough to send his Son to die for you, to pull you out of the pit of your sin, do you think he will be satisfied leaving you at the edge that pit? He has much greater aspirations for you than merely keeping you out of hell. Pursue greatness. Pursue your calling and don't worry whether others think it's spiritual enough—God's opinion is the only one that really matters. God can't wait to start washing that car with you.

Working at Starbucks, I was bothered to see how often the quirkiest customers turned out to be Christians. Many Christians seem to take being "a peculiar people" just a little too literally. Well-intentioned but misguided attempts to be separate from the world have led to a great flood of weirdness, including (but not limited to) building our own Christian theme parks and having our own list of Christian swear words. Being indistinguishable from our culture is a problem, but so is being completely detached from it.

6

Why Are Christians So Weird?

One afternoon as I was coming into work at Starbucks, I saw a guy wandering aimlessly around the parking lot carrying about a dozen red roses. "That's strange," I thought. A couple of minutes later, as I was getting ready to clock on, he came into our store. Seeing him up close, I could tell by his glazed expression that he was not entirely there. He caught my eye, and suddenly a huge smile came over his face as he started walking toward me. Right or wrong, I decided it was high time I headed to the bathroom.

By the time I came back out, he was trying to give a rose to Traci, the partner who was on bar. She politely said, "Thank you, but I don't think my husband would care for that." All the while, I was thinking, "Please don't be a Christian. Please don't be a Christian." I already felt as if I were fighting an uphill battle showing my fellow partners that Christians aren't weird.

"It's not from me," he said. "It's from God."

Yep, he's a Christian.

Traci saw that he meant well and graciously accepted the rose. I later saw it in a glass of water for everyone to enjoy. Looking back, I think I was being hypersensitive. Everyone else understood that he was just a nice guy who was a little confused, not a spokesman for the historic

Christian faith. The real example of Christ that day was Traci, who was well known as a strong believer. Her ever-present smile and kindness said a lot more to my fellow partners than some guy handing out roses. Even still, given all the weirdness I have seen in the name of Jesus, you can't blame me for my concern.

Fitting In

For me to write a book about being normal (radical or otherwise) is a bit ironic. One friend put it nicely by calling me quirky. I used to blame my quirkiness on four years of homeschooling, but I've come to accept that this is who I am. Being a super-Christian appealed to me because it was the only cool thing I had. I dressed like a nerd, and my lowest grade was in PE. Not surprisingly, I lived for Wednesday nights because youth group was the only place I felt normal(ish).

Church is meant to be where quirky, uncouth, overweight, handicapped, broken, and unloved people can be accepted. That's a really good thing, but it can have a downside. My gratitude for being accepted in spite of my weirdness easily transitioned to being proud of not being normal. I know I'm not alone; many Christians have built a theology that promotes weirdness as a biblical virtue. Of course, we don't call it that—we call it things like "hating the world" and "being a peculiar people." I grew up with the impression that if a non-Christian couldn't immediately identify me as a Christian by my unusual clothing or speech, I was ashamed of Jesus.

Many Christians have built a theology that promotes weirdness as a biblical virtue.

Are you ever reluctant to follow God wholeheartedly because you don't want to be associated with weird Christians? Have you ever wondered if you can be a radical Christian and still look normal? And what exactly did Peter mean when he described believers as "aliens and strangers" in this world (1 Peter 2:11)?

A Peculiar People

Being a separate people goes back to Genesis, when God called Abraham out of Ur and made a covenant with him.

> The LORD had said to Abram, "Go from your country, your people and your father's household to the land I will show you.
>
> "I will make you into a great nation,
>   and I will bless you;
> I will make your name great,
>   and you will be a blessing.
> I will bless those who bless you,
>   and whoever curses you I will curse;
> and all peoples on earth
>   will be blessed through you."
>
> So Abram went, as the LORD had told him; and Lot went with him. Abram was seventy-five years old when he set out from Harran (Genesis 12:1-4).

Notice something very important in God's covenant with Abraham. God's goal was not simply to bless Abraham and his descendants. These blessings were supposed to flow through them to the nations (the Gentiles). As near as I can tell, God's blessings are never just for the initial recipients.

In order for Israel to be a blessing to the nations, they had to be different from them. I think that much is evident. How could they be a light to the nations (Isaiah 60:3) if they were just as dark? The problem was that as a small tribe, they were in constant danger of being culturally and morally assimilated into the surrounding nations.[1] I think one of the reasons God brought the Israelites down to Egypt for 400 years was to keep them safe from assimilation. Egyptian racism worked in their favor.[2]

When God delivered Israel from Egypt, he established another covenant—the Mosaic covenant. God reaffirmed Israel's special identity as his family and gave them a long list of rules. Some of these rules were civic laws designed to show them how to operate as a nation. Others were ethical rules that showed them how to act as members of his family. Still other rules told them how to worship God.

God also gave them other rules that were designed to prevent them from being assimilated into the pagan nations. Some of these laws are familiar, such as eating kosher and practicing circumcision. Others are lesser known, such as not sowing two types of seeds in the same vineyard or yoking an ox and a donkey together.[3] In effect, these rules set Israel apart from their neighbors, which helped discourage assimilation.

The Israelites took a while to get good at following these rules, but by the second century BC, many Jews chose to be martyred rather than eat pork. Keeping kosher and following the other Mosaic laws helped them create a uniquely Jewish culture, allowing them to maintain their identity against impossible odds. By the end of the second century AD, Israel ceased to exist as a political nation, yet the people maintained their identity for 1700 years without a homeland. To my knowledge, this is unparalleled in history.

Keeping Separate

Separation did a great job of protecting the Jews from assimilation. So does that mean being separate (and a little odd) could also keep Christians holy? I grew up as an evangelical, and the church did its best to create a nice, safe Christian subculture to help folks like me be as separate from the world as possible.

My favorite Christian artist from that era, Steve Taylor, had a song called "Guilty by Association" that joked about buying milk only from Christian cows. He exaggerated our isolation by the narrowest of margins—I clearly remember my family's Christian Yellow Pages. But I wonder if he was subtly poking fun at himself, because he was a Christian artist and my parents were happy to have me buying his albums instead of listening to Van Halen and Cyndi Lauper. I listened only to Christian music, went to Christian schools or was homeschooled, loved Christian skate night, wore Christian T-shirts, and said *darn it* and *shoot* instead of…other things. In the same way that the kosher rules helped keep Israel safe from the pagan nations, I was definitely safe from the secular world. So was that a good thing or a bad thing?

God told the Israelites to be different as a means to an end—his plan was to bless the entire world through them. If they were not forced to be different from the Gentiles culturally, they would cease to be different from them morally. By the time Jesus came, the Jews had gotten so good at being culturally separate that they forgot about their original mission. The means had become confused with the end.

Living in a Christian subculture is simple. It's far easier to avoid being of the world if you're barely in it.

This didn't end instantly when some Jews became Jesus's disciples. The early believers continued to prize separation so much that after Jesus's resurrection, it took an act of God (literally) to get Peter to share the gospel with Cornelius, a Gentile.[4]

When Cornelius and his family became Christians, the early church had to wrestle with what it meant for Gentiles to become followers of Jesus. Did they have to start acting like Jews and adopt the kosher laws, or could they maintain their Gentile identity?

> Then some of the believers who belonged to the party of the Pharisees stood up and said, "The Gentiles must be circumcised and required to keep the law of Moses."
>
> The apostles and elders met to consider this question. After much discussion, Peter got up and addressed them: "Brothers, you know that some time ago God made a choice among you that the Gentiles might hear from my lips the message of the gospel and believe. God, who knows the heart, showed that he accepted them by giving the Holy Spirit to them, just as he did to us. He did not discriminate between us and them, for he purified their hearts by faith. Now then, why do you try to test God by putting on the necks of Gentiles a yoke that neither we nor our ancestors have been able to bear? No! We believe it is through the grace of our Lord Jesus that we are saved, just as they are" (Acts 15:5-11).

Here's the interesting thing. Nowhere in the New Testament were these Jewish Christians encouraged to separate physically or culturally from the Gentile world. Instead, they were expected to remain in the pagan world without being spiritually polluted by it.

The Bible makes it clear that Gentile Christians (which is most of us) have been grafted in as children of Abraham, and we're now heirs to these promises.[5] This means we have been brought into both their blessing and their responsibility—we're now called to be a blessing to the world. Like the Jews before us, we face the challenge of avoiding assimilation while remaining in the world. As Jesus said, we are in the world, but we must not be of the world.[6]

Living in a Christian subculture is simple. It's far easier to avoid being of the world if you're barely in it. When you have nice, clean boundary lines, you don't have to carefully consider which parts of the culture are acceptable and which ones need to be avoided.

Our Mission

Have you ever been to a Harvest Party? Did you celebrate All-Saints' Eve or Reformation Day? There are other terms for it, but if you grew up as an evangelical, you probably attended some sort of alternative to Halloween. The idea was that Halloween was Satan's holiday, so Christians shouldn't celebrate it.[7] Yet our parents were not so cruel as to deprive us of the candy jackpot, so churches would set up various alternatives where we could dress up as Bible characters and get our treats. It was a great way to keep us safe from the supposedly pagan celebrations and was almost as much fun as trick-or-treating.

In contrast, my church has chosen not to offer a Halloween alternative because we would lose an excellent opportunity to be in the world but not of it. Every Halloween, Marilyn and I take Grace and Sarah trick-or-treating. Rather than locking the front door and turning off the porch light, we throw open our door, serve hot cider, and make our house a warm spot for friends and neighbors who are out trick-or-treating. In our daughters' minds, Halloween isn't about being afraid of ghosts. It's about dressing up, eating candy, and being with friends.

Being a Christian who is in the world but not of it will only get more complicated as the world around us acts less and less Christian. Is that a good thing or a bad thing? Have you noticed that we also have more opportunities than ever before? My daughters have more non-Christian friends than I did at their age. If we cloister ourselves in our churches and tight Christian communities and carefully avoid meaningful connections with the world, we may be safer, but we'll fail in our mission to be a blessing and a light.

Your style (or lack of it) is a function of your personality, not your godliness.

Being weird, different, or separate for its own sake is not a Christian value. Neither is coolness. Your style (or lack of it) is a function of your personality, not your godliness. You *will* seem odd to the world in many ways—that's not optional. But our uniqueness doesn't come from eating special foods, wearing special clothes, or listening to special radio stations. Our uniqueness comes from things like skipping the bachelor party at the strip club, dressing modestly, not finding our meaning in a new car, and not participating in the water-cooler gossip. You don't need to worry about being different culturally. Focus instead on being different morally.

I've been skirting around a word that frightens many of us—*evangelism*. We are Abraham's heirs, and God's great promise was not that all the peoples of earth would be pretty much unchanged by us. We're called to be salt and light, a blessing to the world around us. The good news is that evangelism is far less scary than I used to think.

Witnessing Without Weirdness

I f I couldn't be on bar at Starbucks, I wanted to be in the drive-through. It could be very entertaining. One time, I watched a panhandler drop his pants and moon the entire street. Public nudity is not only illegal but also bad for business, so I called 911. A grateful customer gave me a $20 tip for that.

Another time, I was working with one of my favorite partners, a young Christian-turned-atheist named Sarah. Early in our shift, a middle-aged woman who looked as well-worn as her Astro van pulled up to the window. "Welcome to Starbucks. How are you doing today?" I asked.

"Everyone asks that, but no one really wants to know," she said dully.

She was right. Usually, none of us want to know the answer. But that's not because we're shallow or artificial. If "how are you doing?" literally meant "please share your inner turmoil with me," the question would be intrusive from anyone but close friends. "How are you?" is a culturally appropriate method of demonstrating interest in another person's well-being without being nosy.

This customer was eager to share her inner turmoil with a complete stranger. I didn't see any way out, so I repeated, "No, really, how are you doing?" I was soon hearing about all of the drama in her life, from her childhood to an incident that happened that morning. I nodded and said things like "Wow…Really?…I'm so sorry…" and even "I'll pray for you." Whenever I had to take another order over my headset, she'd pause and then pick right back up when I was done. All the while, she ignored the cars lining up behind her and my glances at them.

I was on the verge of politely asking her to let me serve the next customer when her self-awareness finally kicked in. She pulled ahead about six inches but then started talking again. Another six inches, then more drama. Six more inches, one more thing to tell me. Another six inches…on it went until she could no longer maintain eye contact and just drove off, still talking about her troubles.

We didn't charge the next several customers for their drinks to cool their tempers. Once we got caught up, Sarah said, "I'm really impressed with how you handled Ms. Emotional Baggage Lady. There's no way I could have been that nice."

I had to smile because Sarah had come to work visibly upset. Before we clocked on, I had sincerely asked her how she was doing and listened to some of the heavy stuff she was going through. Atheist or not, she was genuinely grateful for my offer to pray for her.

Sarah didn't know that every time I put on my green Starbucks apron, I prayed a short prayer. "To your glory and with your help." I realized early on that I could be an agent of God's love, not by passing out tracts to customers or preaching to my fellow partners, but by treating everyone who came into the store with dignity. That included the panhandler, the businesswoman, the gay couple, the pastor, and the lady with no sense of boundaries. Even though I failed a lot, God always answered that prayer, and I was able to be salt and light at Starbucks in natural ways, which I enjoyed a lot more than the witnessing of my younger days.

I Hate Witnessing

I went on my first missions trip when I was 14—a six-week outreach in Jamaica. It was the most physically and emotionally grueling thing I had ever done, and I loved every minute of it. Well, not every minute. I was on a performing arts team, which means we performed mediocre dance moves to outdated contemporary Christian music. Unfortunately, I'm extremely uncoordinated (which is why my lowest grade was in PE). But I tried really hard, learned my moves, and stumbled through them for Jesus.

The dancing wasn't the worst part, nor the strange food and the intestinal challenges it caused. The worst part was what happened after each performance. We had to talk to total strangers and try to lead them to Jesus. I hated witnessing on the streets of Seattle with Radical Randy, and I didn't enjoy it any more in the slums of Jamaica. As each song ended, the knot in my stomach grew because I was that much closer to witnessing time. As fear twisted my stomach, my face grew hot with shame. "Am I ashamed of Jesus?" I wondered. "Will he be ashamed of me in heaven?" Fear and guilt battled each other for the last half of every performance—two or three times a day.

That was my defining experience with evangelism— fear mixed with guilt.

My fear usually won, and I did everything I could to avoid witnessing. I knew a little bit about sound equipment, so I'd help pack up our portable sound system. Ironically, in my attempts to avoid witnessing, I developed a reputation of having a "servant's heart." But that was my defining experience with evangelism—fear mixed with guilt.

Does that sound familiar to you? Not the dancing—maybe you had to do skits in Tijuana or door-to-door witnessing in your own neighborhood. But have you ever felt that fear mixed with guilt? Here's the good news. On my journey toward being radically normal, I've discovered just how enjoyable evangelism can and should be.

Attractive Faith

Why was I so scared of talking about Jesus? I was undoubtedly afraid of being rejected, but also, witnessing seemed weird and awkward. I have no problem chatting with a stranger in the checkout line about the weather, but spiritual things are far deeper and more personal. Asking people to talk about God is like asking them to share their inner turmoil with me. It just seems as if we should know each other a little better first.

I think evangelism is frightening to many of us because we think it has to involve talking to complete strangers. Some Christians are really good at that, and I respect them for it, but that doesn't mean all of us are supposed to do the same. Think again about the church being like a body. Each of us is wired uniquely and will naturally take a unique approach to sharing about Jesus. Some people are good at street-corner evangelism (the apostle Paul springs to mind), but they are the exceptions. Another approach to evangelism is much more natural for me.

> Make it your ambition to lead a quiet life: You should mind your own business and work with your hands, just as we told you, so that your daily life may win the respect of outsiders and so that you will not be dependent on anybody (1 Thessalonians 4:11-12).

Similarly, Paul tells people to work hard and be trustworthy "so that in every way they will make the teaching about God our Savior attractive" (Titus 2:10). In both passages, Paul isn't talking about evangelism per se, but about how we pave the way before we start sharing the gospel. Most of us have to win people's respect and make faith attractive before they'll listen to what we have to say.

Think of it this way. Marilyn and I recently tried (unsuccessfully) to sell our house. Let's say you had decided to buy it. Soon after moving in, you would have met the neighbors. You wouldn't have had a choice—houses are ten feet apart in my neighborhood. On one side is a great family. They keep their yard nice, don't let their kids run around screaming all night, and would gladly lend you a couple of eggs. They're also a little different—in a good way. They're kind, they're unselfish, they don't participate in the neighborhood gossip, and they don't seem too worried about keeping up with the Joneses. That part isn't hypothetical; Tristan and Christa are great neighbors and strong Christians.

For argument's sake, let's pretend that on the other side was Radical Randy's family. They don't waste their time on worldly things like yard care or home maintenance. Their cars (working or not) are plastered with Christian bumper stickers. The first time you meet them, they shove a fistful of evangelistic tracts into your hands.

In this hypothetical situation, who is doing a better job of evangelizing? Keep in mind that Tristan and Christa haven't shared the gospel with you yet, but you really like them and want to get to know them better. If they're outside when you pull up to your house, you'll gladly spend a couple minutes chatting with them. But if you see Randy and his family, you'll pull straight into your garage and make sure the door is fully shut before getting out of your car.

As we saw in the last chapter, the church's job is to be a light to the nations. The second Great Commission isn't just for apostles, missionaries, and pastors. You get to help carry it out. But evangelism is a lot easier when it happens in a natural conversation after you've been someone's neighbor for a while, lent them some eggs, and developed an interest in them as people, not as potential converts. You just might find out you have something to learn from them as well.[1]

Common Ground

One Christian author recently wrote that "something is wrong when our lives make sense to unbelievers." Surely that is an overstatement. Some parts of our lives can't make sense to non-Christians, but other parts make perfect sense to them. As I see it, we can take two basic approaches when relating to non-Christians. We can focus on all the stuff that doesn't make sense to them or on the stuff that does make sense.

We don't want less than non-Christians do; we want more.

Which approach do you think will be more effective at winning their respect and making the teachings of God attractive?

Think about all of the common ground we share. Christians and non-Christians want...

> to have healthy relationships
>
> to provide well for their families
>
> to have safe communities and fair governments

to have healthy bodies and live to a ripe old age

to be respected and well-liked

All of these things are straight from the Bible and are desires that God has put in our hearts.[2] Because we share a lot of common ground, the Christian life may not look all that different on the surface from the world's ideals. It makes sense to them. From the outside, we look like good neighbors and ideal employees. But when our non-Christian family, friends, and coworkers scratch below the surface, they discover that we're driven by wholehearted devotion to God and empowered by the Holy Spirit. That is one of the things I mean by radically normal—we aspire to many of the same things non-Christians do, but we approach them in different ways and for radically different reasons.

- Our relationships with friends and family reflect our relationship with God.
- We enjoy possessions and the things of this life without letting them possess us.
- Food and drink bring us real joy, yet we don't use them to fill a void.
- We work hard at our jobs and are ambitious, yet our career isn't our identity.[3]

Notice something important about these differences. We don't want less than non-Christians do; we want more. We enjoy the gifts of this world but don't expect more of them than they can give. This is what makes us different in a good way. Our meaning, hope, and final joy are not entrusted to flimsy things that come and go without a moment's warning. Here's how the apostle Paul put it.

> What I mean, brothers and sisters, is that the time is short. From now on those who have wives should live as if they do not; those who mourn, as if they did not; those who are happy, as if they were not; those who buy something, as if it were not theirs to keep; those who use the things of

the world, as if not engrossed in them. For this world in its
present form is passing away (1 Corinthians 7:29-31).

He didn't mean we shouldn't enjoy the things of this world any
more than meaning we shouldn't love our spouses. He meant that we
should enjoy the temporary things of life while we have them but keep
them in perspective. Take them away, and we haven't lost what is most
important to us. Will this make sense to an unbeliever? Maybe not, but
it might lead to some interesting conversations.

Most of us will be much more effective glorifying God and being a
light to the nations if we start by living a quiet life and having an attractive faith without acting strange. We'll also be much happier that way.

When It's Time to Use Words

I'm not saying that making the gospel attractive is all there is to it.
It's not. I know it's popular to quote Saint Francis of Assisi: "Preach the
gospel at all times. Use words if necessary." The problem is that he never
said that. Francis believed deeply in preaching
the gospel with words but also insisted that it
must be preached through deeds.[4]

We've seen that the apostle Paul talked about
living a quiet life. But he also said, "How, then,
can they call on the one they have not believed
in? And how can they believe in the one of whom
they have not heard? And how can they hear
without someone preaching to them?" (Romans
10:14).

> Words are nec-
> essary. The
> good news that
> God became a
> man and died in
> our place isn't
> exactly intuitive.

Words are necessary. The good news that God became a man and
died in our place isn't exactly intuitive. Witnessing without weirdness
doesn't remove the need to speak. It earns permission to speak. God
puts us in the lives of people he loves, and he helps us win their respect.
It would be a profound tragedy to squander the opportunity and never
share his love and grace with them.

At some point, we all have to face our fears and start talking about
what matters the most to us. But even that doesn't have to be as scary

as it was to me. Perhaps this is one of the best passages on evangelism for those who struggle with witnessing.

> But in your hearts revere Christ as Lord. Always be prepared to give an answer to everyone who asks you to give the reason for the hope that you have. But do this with gentleness and respect, keeping a clear conscience, so that those who speak maliciously against your good behavior in Christ may be ashamed of their slander (1 Peter 3:15-16).[5]

Let's look at some of these phrases a little closer.

Always be prepared. We should be lifelong students of the Bible and seek to understand our faith better. That doesn't mean you need to be a Bible expert. Start by knowing enough to share the key points. Don't worry about being able to answer every question. I've found that saying, "I don't know, but I'll try to find out" can sometimes have a deeper impact than the perfect answer.

Gentleness and respect. In most cases, it's best to wait until you're asked (as Peter said) and then offer your answer. People tend to be more interested in answers to the questions they're asking than the ones you think they should be asking. This is more gentle and respectful than pushing information at them. Folks tend to listen better when they know that you respect them.

The reason for the hope you have. This isn't so much about passing out tracts or doing skits in Tijuana as speaking truthfully about who Jesus is, what he has done, and what he's doing in your life. We all know what it means to be a witness in a courtroom—to give truthful testimony about what you've seen and heard. That's what witnessing meant in biblical times, and it's what it still means. Because of the unique work God has done in your life, you are the very best person to reach some people. Don't underestimate the power of your story.

Keeping a clear conscience...your good behavior. Don't give anyone a reason to accuse you of hypocrisy. People can't argue against your godly actions, so let those back up everything you say.

Slander. Finally, understand that you can say and do everything perfectly and still suffer rejection. Just make sure you're rejected for the right reasons. I can handle being rejected by someone because they're rejecting Jesus as Lord. I just don't want to be so strange or hypocritical that people can't run away fast enough. And I certainly don't want them to reject Jesus because of me.

Here's a challenge. List three people (neighbors, friends, coworkers, family members…) that you wish knew God's grace and start praying for them. Specifically pray for opportunities to be a witness to them. Then just start leading a quiet life (as Paul says in 1 Thessalonians 4:11-12) and be prepared for the opportunities God brings (as Peter says in the passage above).

I don't believe we need to frantically witness to every person we meet for fear that they might die in a car accident the next day. That type of evangelism is based on the false belief that it's all up to you. You know your own story and the way God led you through unlikely yet undeniable paths to bring you home. Never forget that God is also working a unique story in everyone else—a story that may or may not include you sharing the gospel verbally with them or leading them to Jesus. Paul understood that he played just a part in the lives of his converts: "I planted the seed, Apollos watered it, but God has been making it grow. So neither the one who plants nor the one who waters is anything, but only God, who makes things grow" (1 Corinthians 3:6-7).

Always be prepared, never let fear hold you back, and let your message of God's grace be characterized by God's grace. You were not saved by your own works, and neither can you save someone else by your works, "so that no one may boast" (Ephesians 2:8-9).

I really enjoy LarkNews.com, a Christian satire website. One article is titled "Christian Couple Maintains Abstinence Through First Two Years of Marriage." Another classic talks about some Christians who, tired of Third World missions, believe they're called to evangelize the wealthy. Does that sound like what I'm promoting? Am I just trying to remove all of the sacrifice from Christianity and make it too easy? If you aren't thinking that now, you might be before the end of the next chapter.

8

In Defense of Earthly Joys

About a year after starting my job at Starbucks, I heard about a Christian writers' conference in Seattle and decided to go. When I arrived, the speaker was talking about how to write a good "elevator speech," a 30-second pitch for your book that compels the listener to ask for more. "Being a little controversial always helps," he said. Suddenly I had an idea. I wrote it down and played with it a bit. I reread it and chuckled. "I can't say that, can I?" When the speaker invited a few people to share their elevator speech, I raised my hand. He called on me, and I stood up and said, "The world tells us to live for today, and the church tells us to live for eternity. They're both wrong...and they're both right."

Judging by the total silence in the room, I guessed I'd gotten the controversial part down okay. Finally the speaker said, "Yep, that's the idea. I was offended—but I want to know more." I was able to offend and intrigue several more people at the conference, most notably an editor from Harvest House. Thanks to his interest and support, Harvest House later decided to publish this book. That was a good weekend.

Yes, the world tells us to live for today. YOLO (You Only Live Once) is a current buzz phrase used to justify all sorts of questionable decisions. Popular culture encourages us to focus on today without thinking about the long-term consequences, let alone the eternal ones.

The church often tells us to live for eternity, exhorting us to scorn the joys of this life in favor of spiritual things. I recently read a sermon that said we should be alarmed if we desired any pleasure more than prayer and enjoyed any book more than the Bible. A popular devotional suggests that we should trust God so much that we no longer want his blessings, only God himself. A bestselling book mentions a woman who didn't want to be at the theater because she wanted to be at home praying instead. I had no problem with that until the book called her example "convicting."

Are those examples the high-water mark of Christianity? Have we really arrived when praying is more fun than going to a show, reading the Bible is more enjoyable than watching a football game, and a day at church is better than a day at Disneyland?

These two extremes are both wrong—we don't have to choose between living for this life or the next. But they are both right. The closer we get to God, the more robustly we can enjoy both earthly and spiritual things.

To the Joy of the Saints

Joy is one of the central themes of the Bible. When I was doing research for this book, I did an extensive study on the word *joy* and its synonyms, including *happiness*, *pleasure*, and *delight*.[1] I trimmed the list down to the 730 most applicable verses containing those words. That's a lot of verses—more than the number of verses that contain words like *peace*, *grace*, or even *love*.

> I want the words *Christians* and *joyless* to become antonyms.

I printed out all of these verses in ten-point type and set the margins at half an inch, but the list was still 48 pages long. After I printed it, I just sat and thumbed through all those pages, feeling their weight in my hand. Just seeing and feeling how much the Bible had to say about joy changed my theology. For Christians to be so easily and accurately caricatured as joyless is inexcusable. As a result of the months I spent analyzing those verses one by one, I began to sign my letters, "To the glory of God and the joy of the saints." That has become my life mission—I want the words *Christians* and *joyless* to become antonyms.

A Compartmentalized Life

My dad was in the National Guard when I was a kid, so two weeks every year he'd go to Eastern Washington to drive a tank. We always looked forward to his return, hoping he'd bring home some MREs. These nonperishable Meals Ready to Eat are wrapped in a thick brown plastic and include several pouches of foodlike substances. My favorite was the ultra-dense cracker covered in cheese goo. My brother liked the Chicken à la King paste, and I seem to remember my sister enjoying the freeze-dried apples.

Monday morning after his return, the three of us would take an MRE and my dad's mess kit and go hide out under a large rhododendron bush that served as our fort. We'd fight over the mess kit, and I usually won because I was the oldest. I loved the way the handle folded up so neatly over the lid. When opened, the lid became the plate, with a high ridge that divided it into two separate compartments.

I've spent most of my life like that mess kit. In my mind, the spiritual and earthly compartments were ever separated. On the spiritual side were all the things I felt I was supposed to do, and on the earthly side were all the things I actually enjoyed doing.

My Spiritual Compartment	My Earthly Compartment
seeking heavenly joy	experiencing earthly happiness
worshipping	listening to the radio
going to church	playing
reading the Bible	reading Hardy Boys books
tithing	spending my allowance on candy
going on missions trips	going on vacations
praying	talking with friends
being holy	having fun

I didn't think the things in my earthly compartment were bad; they just weren't spiritual, and spiritual is always better, right? That's what I believed before my study of joy.

After printing out those verses about joy, I began to go through each one, making note of who was experiencing joy, whether the Bible approved, and whether the joy seemed to me to be earthly or spiritual. I entered the results into a database and started to analyze the results.[2]

The first surprise was finding that verses about joy occur evenly throughout the Old and New Testaments. The Old Testament isn't all fire and brimstone after all. I was even more surprised to discover that roughly 75 percent of the Old Testament references were to things that I considered earthly joys. In the New Testament, the emphasis shifts almost exclusively to finding joy in things I considered spiritual. That doesn't mean God changed his mind about earthly joy between the Old and New Testaments. As I said in chapter 4, the New Testament was written with the assumption that we'd keep reading and applying the Old. Together they give a complete picture of the life God desires, enjoying all things regardless of whether we think they're earthly or spiritual.

The Old and New Testaments endorse earthly joys once for every two times they endorse spiritual joys. Think about that—if you were to tally up all of the sermons, books, and articles you've heard and seen about seeking spiritual joy, then compare that to the number pertaining to earthly joy, what would the ratio be?

My point is that if God wants us to keep our eyes only on heavenly things, if he wants us to seek only him and not his blessings, if he thinks earthly delights are second best to spiritual ones, then he sure has a funny way of showing it. One hundred sixty-five verses reference unabashed enjoyment of earthly things.

- Entire psalms are dedicated to thanking God for earthly things, such as a good harvest, protection from an enemy, and the restoration of one's health and fortunes.[3]

- We are commanded to enjoy our spouse and delight in each other sexually.[4]

- The Torah commands multiple festivals—huge parties filled with eating and drinking.[5]

- Have you ever felt a thrill when you can make that perfect, witty remark? That's biblical too.[6]

- Paul acknowledges that God richly gives us everything for our enjoyment.[7]

To put it bluntly, God shouldn't be your only happiness. Not because he wouldn't be enough—he's beyond sufficient for an eternity of delight—but because he doesn't want to be. He has filled this world with many things that he longs for us to enjoy, just as any father longs for his children to enjoy good things.

A couple years ago, a friend of mine got a new swing set for his kids and gave me the pieces of the old one. With blood, sweat, tears, and help from a couple friends, I got it set up in my backyard. As we worked on it, Grace and Sarah kept running around us, asking when it would be ready. As soon as we were done, I told them they could play on it. How would I have felt if they'd said, "Oh, that's okay, Daddy. We just want you instead."

I might have said, "I'm glad you love me so much. I love you too, very much. Now get over there and play on the swing set!" Far from being pleased with their maturity, I would have been disappointed that they didn't understand how much I wanted them to enjoy the gift. Do you think maybe God feels disappointed when we fail to delight in his earthly gifts to us?

Of course, that isn't what Grace and Sarah did that day. Before I finished saying, "It's ready," they were already swarming over it with their friends. Scarcely a day goes by (rain or shine) that they're not out there playing on it, and seldom does it fail to elicit a smile from me.

God really likes earthly things. He declared this world very good, and about 80 percent of the biblical references to God enjoying or delighting in something have to do with things he has made (including us) rather than things we think of as more spiritual. More importantly, he became a man and enjoyed created things himself. Jesus is our great example of someone who perfectly enjoyed and indulged in the things of this life without being distracted from his purpose. And through his death, he made it possible for us to enjoy them to the fullest without the sin that corrupts them. We'll get to that soon.

A Unified Life

As I've studied what the Bible has to say about joy and the way it flows so easily between my earthly and spiritual compartments, I've started to view life less like the lid of my dad's mess kit. I see it more like the other side, which was just one big pan. I no longer believe that there are different kinds of joy, just variations of the same thing. All joy comes from God. It has different forms, but it's all his.

Being radically normal means discovering and living a unified life, seeing God and feeling his delight in everything. You can be a spiritual person whether you're enjoying worship or enjoying a football game. In both cases, you're enjoying something God has made.

I'm not saying all joys are exactly the same. Going to a football game is obviously different from attending a worship service. The question isn't which is holier, but which is more appropriate at the time. For instance, I would discourage skipping church every week to watch football. That would be like living on a steady diet of candy, chips, and Coke.

Finding a unified life is far bigger than simply being able to watch a football game without feeling guilty. If you don't genuinely believe that God enjoys you enjoying that game or shopping with friends or reading a novel or whatever else you enjoy, then you're far less likely to invite him to join you in those activities. And if you don't think God is with you, you're far more likely to do ungodly and destructive things.

Imagine being so comfortable with God's pleasure at your pleasure that you spontaneously invite him into everything you do. Imagine being able to scream yourself hoarse for a touchdown one moment and then whisper a "thank you" prayer the next without feeling any separation between the two.

Who throws a better party, your church or your neighbors? If God were to throw a party, what do you think it would be like? As it turns out, God has actually thrown a bunch of parties, and we can learn a lot from them.

9

When God Throws a Party

I don't understand why anybody over the age of ten wouldn't like eggnog. Sweet, thick, rich, and just a little spicy—yum. Eggnog makes me think of Christmas trees, short days and long nights, advent candles, and presents. And now, thanks to working at Starbucks, eggnog has an entirely new association—a piercing, screaming sound. Anyone who has ever steamed eggnog can still hear it ringing in their ears, but the noise is worth the payoff. Coffee and eggnog might seem like a strange combination, but it works well.

When I was in college in the Los Angeles area, I spent one Christmas working in a mall store that sold overpriced personalized merchandise. Between the ultra-commercialization and complete absence of the Christmas spirit, it felt very much like the opening scene of *How the Grinch Stole Christmas*. That was the year I almost abandoned Christmas altogether.

> When I hear Christians say, "Let's put Christ back in Christmas," I get a little uneasy because I'm afraid they won't be happy until Christmas is all Christ and no fun.

In contrast, the holidays were great at Starbucks. As the red cups came out and the Christmas drinks released, customers and partners alike felt the Christmas spirit descend on the store. Part of me knew that the Starbucks corporation was just playing off of our love of tradition to sell more drinks, but the other part didn't care. Just thinking about drinking an eggnog latte on a dark, drizzly December afternoon stirs a longing for winter and its promise of Christmas.

Putting Christ Back in Christmas

Every Christmas, when I hear Christians say, "Let's put Christ back in Christmas," I get a little uneasy because I'm afraid they won't be happy until Christmas is all Christ and no fun. I'm probably being oversensitive, but growing up, I had an impression (*fear* would be a better word) that if I were really spiritual, I would be perfectly happy celebrating Christmas by simply reading the Nativity story in an undecorated room. I wouldn't need a tree, gifts, or special dinner. Shouldn't I give all that money to the poor?

Neither my pastor nor my parents taught me that, but I kept hearing that Christmas needed to be more about Jesus and less about other stuff. But how much more is enough? I talked to one pastor's kid who was required to give her favorite toy away every Christmas. Not just any toy, but her favorite toy. The idea was to teach her that other kids were worse off than she was. That seems to me an effective strategy for teaching your children to resent the church or even God himself. The thought of taking away my daughter's favorite toy in order to teach her a lesson breaks my heart.

On the other hand, I understand why the church works so hard to get the attention back on Jesus. From drunken, gluttonous parties to materialistic gift-giving frenzies, our activities just don't seem that different from the world's. Many families plunge themselves deep into debt to give their kids more gifts than they can possibly appreciate.

My family has avoided that fate—more out of necessity than principle.

Money was especially tight the Christmas I worked at Starbucks. We were able to buy only one nice gift for the family (thanks to waiting in line five hours on Black Friday), a large stuffed animal for Grace and Sarah, and a handful of small items. That year they received more gifts from the rest of the family than from us. Marilyn and I were heartbroken, knowing that our daughters received a tenth of what some kids did…until our precious girls ran up to us and said, "We can't believe how many gifts we got! Thank you!" and then ran off to play with their stuffed animals. I held back tears of thankfulness. That year we decided that regardless of how much money we had in the future, we would never fall into the trap of keeping up with other families. We want to give our girls a few gifts that they will actually enjoy.

Yes, stuff distracts us. The more we acquire, the more we are distracted from the things we already have and from more important things, including the message of hope and joy from our Savior. Holiday fanfare can be distracting, so it's no surprise that obsessive Christians idealize a gift-free Christmas spent serving at a homeless shelter. There's a place for that (I've spent a couple of Christmases serving at homeless shelters), but joyful celebrations have their place as well. In fact, a party is one of God's favorite ways of drawing us to him.

Happy Holy Days!

Scripture is clear—God loves a good party! The Old Testament is filled with more festivals, feasts, and holidays than we have in our calendar. We don't notice them because we don't read the Old Testament all that much, and when we do, we read "holy day" and picture something as enjoyable as a funeral. Without the reception.

Nothing can kill a good party like bringing God into it.

Growing up, my family always had a New Year's Eve party with friends from church. The kids would run around all night, playing, eating, and relishing staying up late. But right at 11:55, the party would screech to a halt, all the kids would be wrangled up, and we'd pray in the New Year. These were all good people who loved Jesus—they weren't self-righteous legalists. They were trying their best to honor God and make him the center of their lives. I get that. But in my young mind, the conclusion I mistakenly drew was that nothing can kill a good party like bringing God into it. Don't tell me you've never had similar thoughts.

Nothing could be further from the truth. Almost all of the biblical holidays (holy days) were parties.

> Nehemiah the governor, Ezra the priest and teacher of the Law, and the Levites who were instructing the people said to them all, "This day is holy to the LORD your God. Do not mourn or weep." For all the people had been weeping as they listened to the words of the Law.
>
> Nehemiah said, "Go and enjoy choice food and sweet drinks, and send some to those who have nothing prepared. This day is holy to our Lord. Do not grieve, for the joy of the LORD is your strength" (Nehemiah 8:9-10).

Obsessive Christians would say, "This is a holy day. Don't laugh, don't eat, don't drink…be solemn and holy" as if it's impossible to have fun and be holy at the same time. But God says (through Nehemiah), "This is a holy day, so have a great time! Break out the marbled beef, open up the bottles, have a party!" Are there times for mourning and fasting? Absolutely, but such solemnity is the exception, not the rule. The Bible refers to fasts about 40 times and to feasts about 140 times. The main focus is on joy. "The joy of the LORD is your strength."

One commentator translates *strength* as *protection*, saying that God's joy is our protection.[1] That makes sense to me. Many people have been led astray with a damnable heresy that removes tangible joy from our faith. Teaching our teenagers to defend the inspiration of Scripture will do little good if they secretly hope it's false. The joy of the Lord defends us and our children from these attacks. God can use joy-filled holidays (and not just the ones listed in the Bible) to draw us closer to him. They need not pull us away.

Joy and Meaning

Passover, Sukkoth, Purim, New Moon festivals…festival after festival is filled with celebration. Why did God command so many parties? First, who doesn't want their kids to have fun? As I've said, the best part of parenting isn't making our kids do their chores or disciplining them, but playing with them or watching them play with each other. But second and more important, the festivals were designed to teach the Jews (especially the children) about their history, God's mighty deeds, and his care for them.

My family enjoys celebrating Passover with other families from our church. This is a recent addition to our holidays, but I love it because Grace and Sarah love it. They love looking for the hidden leaven, munching on the special food, and drinking out of specially decorated cups. Through the fun they are learning all about God's salvation of the Jews in the Exodus and about our redemption through the cross. Jesus is hidden in every nook and cranny of Passover.

> The gospel tells us that every one of us deserves coal in our stocking but gets a pony instead.

I'm trying to apply this same lesson to the way our family celebrates Christmas by looking for opportunities to teach my daughters through our traditions.

- The brightness of Christmas lights or advent candles in a dark room reminds us, "In him was life, and that life was the light of all mankind. The light shines in the darkness, and the darkness has not overcome it" (John 1:4-5).

- The nativity set is a visual reminder of the Incarnation. I vividly remember the one from my childhood and judge all others against it.

- Giving and receiving presents reminds us of God's many gracious gifts, great and small. I'm careful never to ask kids, "Have you been good this year?" It's entirely contrary to the gospel and to the meaning of Christmas. The gospel tells us that every one of us deserves coal in our stocking but gets a pony instead.

- Giving gifts teaches generosity, especially when we find ways to give gifts that cannot be repaid.

- Inviting people over for Christmas dinner teaches our

daughters hospitality. No one should have to celebrate Jesus's birth alone.

- A good, joy-filled Christmas Eve service teaches about Jesus and creates a tradition our children will remember for years. I still remember the stockings filled with candy, tangerines, and mixed nuts that my church gave us every year. I never ate the nuts, but in my mind mixed nuts and Christmas still go hand in hand.

I'm not saying every Christmas tradition must have a meaning pointing back to Jesus's birth. Rather, the elements of fun, joy, and meaning should flow together so seamlessly that we lose all track of which ones convey deep meaning and which are simply fun. If our kids come to think of Christmas as being about gifts, candy canes, *and* Jesus's birth, the candy canes may become the taste of the Incarnation.

This isn't just about Christmas. Christmas is just one of the celebrations we can use to grow spiritually. What are some ways you can infuse meaning into your celebrations of Easter, birthdays, Independence Day, and Halloween?

Partying with God

Of course, many holiday traditions do not honor God—eating to the point of gluttony, drinking to drunkenness, flirting at the office party, or practicing unrestrained materialism. That's one reason God wants to be invited to your parties.

> Beginning with the fifteenth day of the seventh month, after you have gathered the crops of the land, celebrate the festival to the LORD for seven days; the first day is a day of sabbath rest, and the eighth day also is a day of sabbath rest. On the first day you are to take branches from luxuriant trees—from palms, willows and other leafy trees—and rejoice before the LORD your God for seven days (Leviticus 23:39-40).

The key part is "rejoice *before* the LORD," not "*in* the LORD." The Hebrew is literally "before the face of." In other words, we are supposed to have our parties in his presence. This particular festival was a huge harvest festival. The people hung out in tents, enjoyed all the food and wine they had produced, and had an all-around great time.[2] Harvest festivals are a part of most cultures, but in pagan cultures they could get pretty depraved with their fertility rituals and such. God doesn't respond by saying, "Be somber and have a prayer meeting." Instead, he says, "Have a great time in my presence without all of the sorrow and pain that comes with sinful pagan parties."

A happy holy day is a great way to learn about God and have fun. It's also a prime reason radically normal Christians can have a better, more joy-filled party than complacent Christians who ignore God's guidelines and pay the price.

Reflections of Heaven

A good party can have another benefit—it can help prepare you for heaven. In chapter 1, I said that the highlight of my childhood vacations was our day at Disneyland. The night before, I'd usually pray something like this: "Jesus, please don't come back tomorrow." (I also prayed that before my wedding day.) Sure, I wanted to go to heaven, but this was Disneyland!

There are two ways a good Christian parent can respond to that. Chastise the child for being more excited about Disneyland than heaven, or say something like this: "Wasn't today a blast? I had a great time; didn't you? You know what? As amazing as Disneyland is, heaven is going to be even better!"

Which approach do you think is more biblical?

Popular images of sitting on a cloud and playing a harp for eternity look more like hell than heaven to me.

Popular images of sitting on a cloud and playing a harp for eternity look more like hell than heaven to me. Those images meant something to those who created them, but they no longer resonate with most of us today. C.S. Lewis explains it well.

> There is no need to be worried by facetious people who try to make the Christian hope of "heaven" ridiculous by saying they do not want "to spend eternity playing harps." The answer to such people is that if they cannot understand books written for grown-ups, they should not talk about them. All the scriptural imagery (harps, crowns, gold, etc.) is, of course, a merely symbolic attempt to express the inexpressible. Musical instruments are mentioned because for many people (not all) music is the thing known in the present life which most strongly suggests ecstasy and infinity. Crowns are mentioned to suggest the fact that those who are united with God in eternity share His splendour and power and joy. Gold is mentioned to suggest the timelessness of Heaven (gold does not rust) and the preciousness of it. People who take these symbols literally might as well think that when Christ told us to be like doves, He meant that we were to lay eggs.[3]

God knows we can't understand heaven, so he uses analogies that speak to us. When I talk to my daughters about heaven, I compare it to Disneyland, not because heaven is a big amusement park, but because it's the greatest thing they can imagine. Likewise, God compares heaven to something I can easily understand—a party.

> On this mountain the LORD Almighty will prepare
>   a feast of rich food for all peoples,
> a banquet of aged wine—
>   the best of meats and the finest of wines.
> On this mountain he will destroy
>   the shroud that enfolds all peoples,
> the sheet that covers all nations;
>   he will swallow up death forever.
> The Sovereign LORD will wipe away the tears
>   from all faces;

he will remove his people's disgrace
   from all the earth.
The LORD has spoken (Isaiah 25:6-8).

Harps and clouds? No thanks. A banquet with the best food and wine money can buy? Hallelujah! Will heaven literally have filet mignon and aged Bordeaux? I have a hard time imagining that animals will have to die in heaven for us to dine, so it might not be exactly literal, but this picture of heaven uses things I can understand to help me get excited about things I cannot.

The best image of heaven I've ever experienced was a composite of three weddings I was honored to officiate. The first was Caleb and Teresa's wedding. Caleb was from Mexico, so they had a bilingual wedding, which I co-officiated with Caleb's Spanish-speaking pastor. At the reception afterward, as I saw the mixture of languages, cultures, and food, I was overcome by this preview of the wedding feast of the Lamb, which will include "every nation, tribe, people and language" (Revelation 7:9).

The second was the wedding of my friends Dave and Elizabeth. I had walked with Dave as God healed and restored him after his first marriage, so their wedding was deeply personal to me. They were both trophies of God's grace and redemptive power. Similarly, heaven will be one long display of redemption. As a bonus, Dave had worked at a popular pub and Elizabeth sang in a band, so the reception was filled with people who knew how to have fun but without the excess that often mars such celebrations.

The third wedding was for one of my best friends, Israel, and his bride, Jen. They had rented a small retreat center for two days prior to the wedding so all of their friends and family could eat together, decorate together, and just enjoy hanging out. By the time the wedding came, we shared a tangible sense of community.

Together, those three weddings have given me a taste of heaven that I'm genuinely excited for—every nation joining in a huge party, celebrating God's grace and redemption as a big family. I've come to believe that celebrations are appetizers for the feast of a lifetime. The doors to *that* banquet hall are closed to me for now, but if these treats are any indication of what's to come…oh, wow!

If you were to offer toddlers a choice between a cheap hot dog of questionable origin and a tender, perfectly cooked and seasoned filet mignon, they would probably choose the hot dog. Good taste is cultivated. I'm learning that when I focus on earthly joys at the expense of spiritual joys, I'm demonstrating just how underdeveloped my tastes are. When we fail to cultivate heavenly tastes, we're the ones missing out.

In Defense of Spiritual Joys

Another reason I liked working in the Starbucks drive-through was the view out the window. Beyond Riverside Drive and past an assortment of banks and strip malls stood the foothills, green year-round thanks to our beloved evergreen trees. I didn't fully appreciate them until I went to school in Southern California and lived without green 11 months out of the year. Beyond the foothills rose Mount Baker, snowcapped even in the middle of summer. I've seen many beautiful things in my life, but few compared to seeing our mountain painted pink by the sunset and flanked by a silver moon.

Growing up in the Pacific Northwest, I've always been surrounded by beauty—mountains, forests, rivers, and the San Juan Islands. Washington and Oregon frequently appear on lists of the least churched states in the Union, and sociologists suggest that is because nature provides spiritual experiences here without church. I know that my most powerful encounters with God usually happen in nature. People who live in places like this understand the beauty and majesty of God in ways that other people may not. On the other hand, perhaps people from the Great Plains understand his vastness as I cannot, and city dwellers might see his face in humanity better than I do.

We've talked about enjoying earthly things without guilt, but it would be a tragedy if you used that as an excuse to neglect spiritual joy and not seek God himself. My hope and prayer is that what you read here makes you long for God more, not less. I wrote earlier that God should not be your only joy. But he must be your ultimate joy—the source of every happiness and the reality behind the glimpses.

I've enjoyed skydiving and white-water rafting, but rare moments of feeling God's undeniable presence have brought me deeper thrills than anything else I've experienced. Prayer in the middle of great turmoil has filled me with peace, comfort, and perspective that the best counsel of friends could not match. Quiet moments in nature with God have ushered in moments of happiness so sublime that they cannot be shared without cheapening them.

If God has filled this world with so much joy, how much more must knowing him bring joy?

Even still, I'm not sure that I'm the best one to talk about enjoying God and his presence. In my experience, those moments I described are rare and hard to come by. It's much easier for me to find joy in earthly things than spiritual things. Seeking spiritual joy is far from natural or automatic for me. Most of the time it's hard work. This isn't false humility—conversations with others have shown me that some people have an easier time seeking and enjoying spiritual things than I do. Perhaps this chapter will seem elementary to you, but if you also struggle to enjoy God, I hope my experiences can help you. Here are four things that have been helpful for me.

Looking for Reflections

In the last chapter, we saw that earthly celebrations can provide glimpses of heaven. In the same way, properly enjoying this life helps me seek spiritual things. On days when enjoying God loses concrete meaning and spiritual practices feel more like sacrifice than joy, I remember all the joy in this life. If God has filled this world with so much joy, how much more must knowing him bring joy? If God delights in me, might I also delight in him? This doesn't magically make prayer as much fun as watching a football game, but it gives me hope that prayer will bring me joy in the long run.

Delayed and Instant Gratification

One of the best parts about working at Starbucks was the generous coffee benefit. Every week we received one pound of coffee. Before and after each shift we'd get a free drink or two, and during our shift there was no limit. Unfortunately, my waistline began to reflect this benefit. Fortunately, Marilyn worked at a health club at the time, so I used the free membership to work off my Starbucks pounds.

Some people talk about how much they love exercise—feeling the burn, getting high on endorphins, and all that. I'm not one of those people. I hate exercise. Each week I'd go to a group weight lifting class and try to keep up with the masochistic German instructor. The only thing that kept me going was counting down the minutes until I could relax in the sauna. I loved the sauna. It was actually good for sermon writing—something about the sound-dampening steam, stifling heat, and cool tiles allowed me to wander through the dense forest in my mind and find order.

Every time I went to the gym I had to fight the temptation to skip the workout and head straight to the sauna. I gave in a couple of times, telling myself I was short on time and needed to start brainstorming on the sermon. The funny thing is, it didn't work without the misery of exercise. The thoughts that normally jumped out at me remained hidden behind the trees.

So I exercise—not because I enjoy it, but because I enjoy the results. I like not getting winded by a trip up the stairs. I like the self-discipline that spills over into other areas of my life. I like the extra energy I have for work and playing with Grace and Sarah. I keep these things in my mind as I suffer. I keep reminding myself that I exercise in order to improve the chances of playing with my future great-grandchildren.

All joy lies somewhere along a spectrum. On the left side of the spectrum is instant gratification, and on the right side is eternal joy in God's presence (the ultimate delayed gratification). Somewhere in the middle is long-term earthly joy. None of these joys are wrong, but each has its proper time and place. Even instant gratification can be entirely appropriate, as when we are refreshed by ice cold water on a hot day.

The problem comes whenever we seek one of these joys at the expense of the others. Many Christians spend most of their energy on the left side, seeking instant gratification and the immediate payoff. This is like skipping the workout and heading straight for the sauna, followed by a Venti Caramel Frappuccino to cool down. Complacent, nearsighted Christianity is all too willing to live for today at the expense of eternal happiness. On the other hand, obsessive, farsighted Christianity places all the emphasis on spiritual joy at the expense of earthly happiness. It can be like a personal trainer who makes you feel guilty if you don't run one more mile, lift five more pounds, or avoid eating anything with fat or sugar in it.

Spiritual Disciplines

To embrace spiritual joy, we frequently have to choose long-term happiness over instant gratification. Throughout the Bible and church history, we've been encouraged to do that through various spiritual disciplines, such as praying, reading the Bible, embracing solitude, and fasting. Living as we do in an age of instant gratification, these have naturally fallen from favor. Spiritual discipline would be a lot easier if it had the same immediate payoff as a gourmet chocolate cake. Rather than trying to pretend the disciplines are fun, I've found that focusing on the long-term benefits helps me get started.

There are many disciplines, but I want to focus on five that are good to begin with—solitude and silence, prayer, fasting, Bible reading, and church participation. Many excellent books on spiritual discipline are available, so I don't need to repeat what they say. I'll just give you a quick summary from my perspective (see appendix 2 for more resources).

Solitude and Silence

The constant barrage of noise in our modern world leaves little room in our minds for God. It takes intentional effort to slow down, be alone, turn off the phone, quiet the chatter in our head, and just be.

> Be still, and know that I am God;
> I will be exalted among the nations,
> I will be exalted in the earth (Psalm 46:10).

Practicing silence and solitude teaches you to slow down and enjoy God. I think that's one of the reasons nature is such an effective place for me to experience God—I'm by myself without distractions. Here is how to practice this. Find ten minutes a day to be alone and quiet with God. Take a walk without headphones or drive home without the radio on. Notice how strange the quiet feels and realize how conditioned to noise you've become. Ask God to quiet your heart.

Prayer

Prayer can include structured times of asking for God's intervention as well as free-form conversations with him. Both are important. I love having a running conversation with God throughout the day and asking for his help as situations come up. Staying focused through my times of structured prayer is difficult for me—which is why it's so important. Practice both types and pay closer attention to the one that comes less naturally.

Fasting

Fasting used to play a large role in the Christian life, but it's all but ignored in modern America. Why is that? Because it requires not eating! Yet try as I might, I can't get around the fact that Jesus expects us to fast.

> John's disciples came and asked him, "How is it that we and the Pharisees fast often, but your disciples do not fast?"
>
> Jesus answered, "How can the guests of the bridegroom mourn while he is with them? The time will come when the bridegroom will be taken from them; then they will fast" (Matthew 9:14-15).

When I finally started obeying, I learned that fasting did some things that nothing else could. For instance, fasting gives my prayers greater focus because it costs me something. Fasting also helped me realize that I was supposed to be in control of my body, not the other way around. (Fasting has taught me another lesson, one of the most important of my life, but I'm saving that for chapter 16.)

Paradoxically, fasting also helps me enjoy earthly things more. My family has recently started observing Lent by giving up something that's perfectly acceptable (such as sugar) for the 40 days prior to Easter. I don't need to tell you how much Grace and Sarah look forward to their Easter baskets! There was another unexpected benefit. We follow the tradition that takes Sundays off from the fast, so my daughters also look forward to their hot chocolate and dessert every Sunday during Lent.[1] I can't tell you how much I love knowing that my daughters have come to associate Sunday with the joy of hot cocoa and marshmallows.

Bible Reading

I recently read about a survey that indicated that the best predictor of your ability to resist temptation isn't church attendance, prayer, or participation in an accountability group. People are most likely to resist temptation if they read their Bibles four times a week or more. That surprised me at first, but it lines up perfectly with what Scripture says about itself.

> How can a young person stay on the path of purity?
>   By living according to your word.
> I seek you with all my heart;
>   do not let me stray from your commands.
> I have hidden your word in my heart
>   that I might not sin against you (Psalm 119:9-11).

There is no substitute for spending time reading, studying, and meditating on God's Word. Through it, God speaks to us and fills us with hope, wisdom, joy, and strength. Bear in mind that on Judgment Day, you won't be able to blame your pastor for your lack of spiritual knowledge—you have a Bible and the ability to study it for yourself as well as the Holy Spirit's guidance.

Church Participation

Church as a part of the Christian life has declined significantly in past decades. People ask, "Do I have to go to church in order to be a Christian?" Technically, no you don't. But technically, being married doesn't mean you have to have sex either. Yet if there is no intimacy, something very important (and desirable) is missing. If you're not committed to a healthy, local church body, it's to your detriment and loss.[2]

Just as the health benefits keep me exercising when I don't want to, knowing that these disciplines will bring me joy keeps me going. Also like physical exercise, they become easier and more enjoyable the more I practice them. My tastes become more attuned to enjoying spiritual things, and I feel the loss when I skip these disciplines.

A couple of weeks ago, I was getting pretty anxious about finishing this book on time and was struggling with a chapter that wouldn't come together. Marilyn wisely suggested that I take a break from writing to spend time with God. At first, I objected that I didn't have the time, but I knew she was right. It was amazing how much a walk around a pond did to remind me how much I enjoyed being with him. Through silence and solitude, a little praying, and meditating on a verse, God reminded me that my writing was about him and what he wanted to speak to me, not my ceaseless striving. It was as if he said, "I've missed you," and I realized I missed him too.

Experiencing God in Worship

Did you notice that I didn't talk about worship as a spiritual discipline? I was saving it. This is the one that has had the greatest impact on me personally.

Growing up in Charismatic and Pentecostal churches, the emphasis was always on experiencing God through worship, which was thought to be synonymous with singing songs. The problem was that I just didn't enjoy worship as much as everyone else. I assumed that something must be wrong with me, so I kept trying harder. I'd focus on the lyrics as best I could. Sometimes I'd find unintentional contradictions—is the greatest thing in my life supposed to be knowing God, loving him, or serving him?[3] Whenever I mentioned these to someone, I just got a blank stare. But every once in a while, I'd discover something new about God during worship, and then I'd really experience his presence.

Have you ever read a book that answered deep questions you didn't even know to ask? That happened to me when I read Gary Thomas's book *Sacred Path-ways*. The very short version is that each of us is wired differently, so we worship and experience God's presence in different ways. He lists nine biblical pathways to worshipping. All of them should play a part in our Christian walk, but some will be more meaningful for you than others. Which of these pathways, or spiritual temperaments, resonate the most with you?

Enough is one of the most devastating words in the Christian's vocabulary.

> intellectual—loving God with the mind
>
> contemplative—loving God through adoration
>
> enthusiast—loving God with mystery and celebration
>
> caregiver—loving God by loving others
>
> activist—loving God through confrontation
>
> ascetic—loving God in solitude and simplicity
>
> traditionalist—loving God through ritual and symbol
>
> sensate—loving God with the senses
>
> naturalist—loving God out of doors

Thomas's book set me free. I finally understood why singing songs did little to help me worship, but a walk in the woods ushered me into God's presence. And nothing was wrong about really enjoying God by loving him with my mind.

How about you? Have you ever felt as if something were wrong with you because of how you experience God? Denominations and churches tend to be built around specific pathways, so unless you happen to be in a church that fits your pathways, you may feel like something of a misfit. Could discovering your pathways help you to genuinely enjoy God more?

Is It Enough?

How do we know if we're doing all of these spiritual practices enough? If we're seeking spiritual joy enough? I used to struggle with this a lot. If I read one chapter in the Bible, I felt bad for not reading two. If I prayed for ten minutes, I felt unspiritual for not praying for twenty. Sometimes it was easier not to start than to feel guilty for stopping.

Enough is one of the most devastating words in the Christian's vocabulary. How can you know when you're doing enough? It's simple. You are never doing enough. There are always more prayers to pray and verses to read. This is one of the most neglected aspects of grace—even at our very best, we can never practice the spiritual disciplines enough. In the end, it's still about relying on God's grace and trusting Jesus to do what we cannot. Spiritual health isn't found in obsessively trying to do it all but gratefully playing the part he has given us.

So how can we tell whether we're playing our part? How do we avoid being complacent under the guise of grace? By looking to scriptural examples of balancing earthly and spiritual joys. As we saw in the last chapter, God commands us to fast and to feast. Obedience and joy require that we balance these.

Maybe *balance* isn't the best word. It implies finding a fixed point between two extremes. Have you ever tried to balance on top of a post? You don't keep your balance by staying perfectly still. You stay balanced by making countless little adjustments to counter wind, muscle fatigue, and friends who are trying to push you off. Likewise, the balance between earthly and spiritual joy is anything but static. Most of the time, earthly joys capture our attention and we need to lean into spiritual things in order to keep balanced. But the minute we start to feel confident in our spiritual disciplines, self-righteousness and legalism begin to pull us the other way, so we need to embrace earthly joys more.

I've found that the closest I can come to balance is this radically normal ebb and flow of earthly joys and spiritual disciplines. One of the reasons why consistent spiritual practices are so helpful is that they serve as ongoing reminders to keep focusing our eyes on God and eternity. They create a cycle—enjoy…abstain…enjoy. Have times of fasting, Scripture, prayer, and worship, interwoven with times of celebration and enjoyment. This is what I see in Scripture and what has worked in my life. It's not stagnant perfection, but an ongoing work of God's grace.

Again and again, we come back to joy. The better we know God and do what he wants us to do, the more joy we'll find, both in the here and now and the hereafter. That's the truth we'll explore in the next chapter—obedience that brings joy.

11

Happy Holiness

One fine summer afternoon, I was working in the drive-through at Starbucks and had a customer order a Venti sugar-free, heavy-cream, no-whip Caramel Frappuccino Light. Allow me to translate. That's a 20-ounce Frappuccino made with sugar-free caramel syrup, but instead of milk, she wanted unwhipped whipping cream. But (and she was very clear about this) she didn't want any whipped cream on it.

As she pulled up to the window, I was curious to see what sort of person would order a Venti heavy-cream Frappuccino. I don't want to be insensitive, so I'll just say she looked the part. I chatted with her as her drink was being made and asked (as casually as I could) why she didn't want any whipped cream on her drink.

"It's because of the sugar in the whipped cream. I'm on a diet that lets me have as much fat as I want but no sugar."

As I handed it to her, I said, "Just so you know, the base syrup we use has a little bit of sugar in it. Not much, but a little."

"Oh," she said. "That must be why I haven't lost any weight."

I'm rarely left speechless, but words failed me. I just grunted some sort of goodbye as she drove off. Let me get this straight—that drink had almost 70 grams of fat, and she thought a couple of grams of sugar was the reason she wasn't losing any weight?

Even now I have to wonder. Did she really believe the sugar was the reason for her weight problem? Somewhere deep down, she must have known that losing all that weight might require a little more work than skipping the whipped cream on a 750-calorie drink. It's easy to point fingers because her problem was so visible, but all of us crave quick fixes to deep problems. And quick fixes usually make problems worse.

When I was young (but old enough to know better), I hated to stop playing when I had to go to the bathroom, so I'd just pee my pants. Cold days were the worst. I vividly remember that feeling of having to pee so bad but not wanting to go inside. There were a few glorious moments when I enjoyed the relief and the newly acquired warmth. But the relief was short-lived. Soon the warm turned to cold, and then came the chafing of my skin against the cold, wet denim, followed by that distinctive smell. I continued doing that until the third grade, my only year in public school. The shame of peeing my pants on a field trip motivated me to start using the bathroom.

Sin is the moral equivalent of peeing our pants. It begins as a short-sighted solution to a genuine problem or a short-lived pleasure at the expense of long-term happiness. I basically see God's rules like him telling us to use the bathroom.

The Big Lie

Why do we choose to sin? Because at the time, we believe we'll be happier doing what's wrong. That, of course, is a lie. It's not just any lie—it's a repackaging of the first recorded lie. The same lie is repeated down through the ages, telling us that sin is more fun than righteousness.

> Now the serpent was more crafty than any of the wild animals the LORD God had made. He said to the woman, "Did God really say, 'You must not eat from any tree in the garden'?"
>
> The woman said to the serpent, "We may eat fruit from the trees in the garden, but God did say, 'You must not eat fruit from the tree that is in the middle of the garden, and you must not touch it, or you will die.'"

"You will not certainly die," the serpent said to the woman.
"For God knows that when you eat from it your eyes will
be opened, and you will be like God, knowing good and
evil" (Genesis 3:1-5).

Do you see what Satan is doing? Do you see his tactic? He's questioning God's goodness. "Here's this great gift," says Satan, "but God doesn't want you to have it. He's holding out on you." This lie works so well that he continues to use it again and again. Too often, Satan's lie seems plausible. If you were to ask 100 random people, "Who do you think is more fun, the devil or God?" who would get more votes? (If no one was watching, how would you vote?)

I once heard about the dean of a Christian college who routinely denied reasonable requests simply because he thought being told no was good for the students. Is that how you picture God? I think he must be troubled that so many people see him that way, especially since Jesus was so clear about what the Father is like.

Which of you, if your son asks for bread, will give him a
stone? Or if he asks for a fish, will give him a snake? If you,
then, though you are evil, know how to give good gifts to
your children, how much more will your Father in heaven
give good gifts to those who ask him! (Matthew 7:9-11).

This picture of God profoundly impacts me because I know how much I delight in giving good gifts to Grace and Sarah. It also helps me understand why God says no so often. How would I respond if my daughters asked to play with my sharpest kitchen knife? How should God respond when we ask for a snake instead of a fish? I'm convinced that we ask him for a lot of snakes, stones, thorns, and rabid squirrels because we're too foolish to know how harmful they are. Do his refusals mean he's a killjoy or that he's a loving and protective father?

My daughters don't always understand or like what I do as their father. When Grace was eight months old, she got a deep gash on her lip. The doctor said she needed stitches in order to avoid a scar. If she were a boy, a scar might have been fine, but not for my little princess.

Do you know how they give stitches to a baby who is incapable of understanding the purpose behind the pain? By holding her down against her will and forcing her to lie perfectly still.

There were enough nurses to hold her, but I insisted on helping. I wouldn't let her go through that alone. I still get choked up when I remember pinning her arms down and trying to speak calming words as I struggled to hold back the tears. If I can love my daughter in ways that are incomprehensible to her, how much more can I believe that God is indeed good and compassionate in all he does as my Father? Maybe even his rules are good and perfect gifts.

> **"Satan, not Christ, is the great teetotaler, the joyless puritan, the cosmic killjoy."**
>
> —LOUIS MARKOS

In the movie *Inception*, Leonardo DiCaprio's character engages in corporate espionage by sneaking into people's dreams to steal sensitive information. One client, however, wants him to do something everyone thinks is impossible—implant an idea in someone's mind. That got me thinking. If I could implant just one idea into everyone's mind, what would it be? Just this—"God's commands bring joy." One idea to contradict that one lie. I want people to believe at a gut level that God's rules will bring joy, not misery. I don't have that technology, so I wrote this book instead.

Rotten Fruit

One of the best things I've ever read about sin is C.S. Lewis's *Screwtape Letters*. It's written as a collection of letters from an experienced demon, Screwtape, to a new tempter. Lewis helps us think differently about the nature of sin and Satan. Gone are the comic images of horns and pitchforks or the suave and urbane Satan. Instead we see Satan and his demons as they really are. I once listened to a set of lectures about Lewis, and something the lecturer said struck me so hard that I went back and listened to it over and over again and wrote it out verbatim. That Sunday, my sermon was inspired by these words.

> Lewis understood, as many Christians even may not, that it's Satan, not Christ, who hates the physical appetites and

the proper joy linked to them. It's Satan, not Christ, who is the great teetotaler, the joyless puritan, the cosmic kill-joy…"The thief comes only to steal, kill, and destroy; but I come that you might have life, and have it to the full."[1]

If Satan is more fun than God, it's only in the same way that the drug dealer handing out free samples to junior high students is more fun than the police officer trying to chase him away. The fun is nothing more than the bait to lead us into misery. Screwtape writes about this.

> [God] is a hedonist at heart. All those fasts and vigils and stakes and crosses are only a façade. Or like the foam on the seashore. Out at sea, out in His sea, there is pleasure, and more pleasure. He makes no secret of it; at His right hand are "pleasures for evermore"…
>
> He has filled his world full of pleasures. There are things for humans to do all day long without his minding in the least—sleeping, washing, eating, drinking, making love, playing, praying, working. Everything has to be twisted before it is any use to us.[2]

For reasons both financial and philosophical, Marilyn and I are members of a local gleaners group. Gleaners gather and share past-date food donated by local grocery stores and restaurants. It's like recycling but for food. Members sort through the food, putting like foods together and picking out food that's too rotten to be redeemed. All the rotten food is thrown into a big trash can and taken home by some members to feed to their chickens.

Sin is not a random list of fun things God doesn't want us to do.

Try to imagine that trash can, filled with moldy strawberries, smashed tomatoes, and other things you can't quite identify. Think of the smell after it has sat in the sun and stewed in its juices. Think of the cloud of fruit flies. Now imagine pulling out a handful of that goop and shoving it in your mouth. My gag reflexes just kicked in.

That is a picture of sin. Sin is not a random list of fun things God doesn't want us to do. Rather, our Creator, who loves us and knows how we tick, says, "Here is what will destroy you and those around you, what will destroy your relationships with other people and your relationship with me. Let's call it sin. Don't do it. It's rotten, it's poison, it's sickness—run away from it."

When the Bible tells me not to cheat on my wife, not to get drunk, not to love this world or the things of this world, I see God standing in front of that trash can saying, "Don't eat this! You think you want it, but you really don't." And when the Bible tells me to love my neighbors, to forgive others, and to be generous, I see him handing me a perfect peach—ripe, sweet, juicy, without a single bruise—saying, "This is what you really want. This is what I want for you."

The point is that wholehearted devotion to God is the best path to joy. Real joy. Earthly joy and spiritual joy. Joy in this life and joy in the next. It's not necessarily the shortest or easiest path to joy, but it's the path to the deepest, most permanent joy. By the way, there wasn't a sharp distinction between temporal and eternal joy in biblical thought. That was a later, nonbiblical addition. In her book *God and the Art of Happiness*, professor and theologian Ellen Charry shows how Greek philosophy (especially Neoplatonism) unduly influenced the early church to emphasize eternal joy at the expense of earthly. This unbiblical influence is with us still.[3]

Duty or Delight?

It seems to me that complacent Christians don't believe that all of God's rules are meant to bring earthly joy, which means they don't believe that God genuinely wants our best. Our actions usually prove what we really believe. If we believed that obedience brings joy, we wouldn't need to be told to do the right thing. Instead, we see obedience as the spiritual equivalent of eating our lima beans. (I detest lima beans.)

Obsessive Christians don't really believe that obedience brings earthly joy either, so they obey God out of joyless obligation. Obsessive Christians keep shoving the lima beans down their throats because they're supposed to. They believe they have to suffer now in order to be happy in heaven.

When we're radically normal Christians, we obey God because we know that obedience brings joy and disobedience brings misery. Does that sound too self-focused? Many Christians assume it must be better to obey God out of a sense of duty than in hopes of reward. C.S. Lewis didn't think so.

> If there lurks in most modern minds the notion that to desire our own good and to earnestly hope for the enjoyment of it is a bad thing, I suggest that this notion has crept in from Kant and the Stoics and is no part of the Christian faith. Indeed, if we consider the unblushing promises of reward and the staggering nature of the rewards promised in the Gospels, it would seem that our Lord finds our desires, not too strong, but too weak.[4]

Far more often than not, God calls us to obey for our own sake rather than out of duty. Here are just a few examples.

> Keep his decrees and commands, which I am giving you today, so that it may go well with you and your children after you and that you may live long in the land the LORD your God gives you for all time (Deuteronomy 4:40).

The longest chapter in the Bible is dedicated to knowing and obeying God's Law. This is how it begins.

> Happy are those whose way is blameless,
>   who walk in the law of the LORD.
> Happy are those who keep his decrees,
>   who seek him with their whole heart, who also do
>   no wrong,
>   but walk in his ways (Psalm 119:1-3 NRSV).

The Bible is filled with sacrifice and suffering for the sake of Jesus, yet he unashamedly calls us to die so that we may live and give up so that we may gain more.

Then Jesus said to his disciples, "Whoever wants to be my

disciple must deny themselves and take up their cross and follow me. For whoever wants to save their life will lose it, but whoever loses their life for me will find it. What good will it be for someone to gain the whole world, yet forfeit their soul? Or what can anyone give in exchange for their soul? For the Son of Man is going to come in his Father's glory with his angels, and then he will reward each person according to what they have done (Matthew 16:24-27).

Never forget that he sacrificed himself "for the joy set before him" (Hebrews 12:2). Shouldn't our obedience and sacrifice be motivated by joy as well?

Yes, we also obey in order to glorify God. As Jesus said, "let your light shine before others, that they may see your good deeds and glorify your Father in heaven" (Matthew 5:16). And **We never get** yes, God occasionally commands things simply **away with sin.** "because I said so" (such as when God told Israel to march around Jericho for seven days). Yet we have been listening to Satan's lie that God is miserly for so long, we need to rediscover the Bible's emphasis on obedience for the sake of joy.

Sin's Slavery

We need to stop thinking of sin as something we get away with and start seeing it as something we're saved from. We never get away with sin. We may be forgiven and restored, but sin always damages us and the ones we love.

We often don't understand how sin will bring misery. The first step to being free from sin is to want to be free. Here's a two-step process I've used when I can't understand how obeying God will make me happier.

Think Through the Consequences

I'd like to invent a contraption I'd call the Consequence Inverter. This is how it would work. Let's say I buy myself an expensive gadget we can't afford—without telling Marilyn. The Consequence Inverter would make me suffer all the consequences before opening the box. I'd have to tell Marilyn about my dishonesty and spend months rebuilding trust. I'd have to pay off the credit card and explain to my daughters why we can't afford to buy them new school clothes. After all that, I'd be allowed to play with my new toy. But the most important feature of the Consequence Inverter would be that I could return the gadget at any point and undo all of the consequences.

If you had a Consequence Inverter, how often do you think you'd push through all the negative consequences so you could "enjoy" a bad choice? That's the purpose of this step—asking God (and perhaps a couple of wise friends or your pastor) to help you see the consequences of that sin you're hanging on to. More often than not, you'll be able to see how obedience will indeed make you happier.

As I clearly understand the consequences of sin and how easily we slide from little sins to big sins, sin becomes much less appealing. I know that any sin, left unchecked, can lead to hell on earth. For instance, when I'm tempted to gaze at an attractive woman other than my wife, I know that it won't be enough. Eventually I'll start looking at questionable images on my computer. That will lead to unquestionably bad images. If I continue on that path, it would cost me everything that means anything to me: my relationships with God, my wife, my family, and my church. Knowing all that, whenever I'm tempted to take that first look, I remind myself, "That's the doorway to hell on earth." I'm not being dramatic—I've seen it happen to others far too many times.

Trust God More than Yourself

What if we can't see the negative consequences? Just as my eight-month-old daughter couldn't understand why I let the doctor poke her with a needle, I fully expect that I won't always understand God's ways (what with him being God and me not). That is where trusting God comes in.

> Trust in the LORD with all your heart
> and lean not on your own understanding;
> in all your ways submit to him,
> and he will make your paths straight (Proverbs 3:5-6).

This passage doesn't discourage critical thinking. The entire book of Proverbs praises wisdom and clear decision making. "Lean not on your own understanding" means that whenever your understanding doesn't line up with what God says, you trust him more than yourself. It means you assume that he knows more than you do.

Many Christians don't believe that the entire Bible is "God-breathed" and feel free to dismiss the parts that they don't like or understand. But isn't it convenient that the supposedly uninspired parts just happen to be the parts they don't agree with? I mean, why shouldn't the "God is love" part be man-made and hell be the only true part?

I don't understand the entire Bible, and I honestly don't like parts of it, but I start with the assumption that God's ways are above mine, and I seek to learn what he has to teach me even in those parts. When I approach Scripture with that humility, I frequently discover that the parts I like the least are the ones I need the most. For instance, I struggle with how often the psalmists attack their enemies so vindictively. But C.S. Lewis points out, "If the Jews cursed more bitterly than the Pagans this was, I think, in part because they took right and wrong more seriously."[5] Those psalms help me realize how casual I am about sin's scourge in the world.

At its core, all sin is a type of unbelief, of not trusting God and his character. We believe we'll be happier and healthier ignoring him and doing things our way. Trusting God more than yourself begins with one of the best, most honest, and most powerful prayers in the Bible: "I do believe; help me overcome my unbelief!"[6] You may not yet be ready to get rid of your sin, and you may not yet believe that obedience will bring joy, but you're choosing to submit to God's will instead of your own.

Holiness isn't an obligation as much as a benefit of following Jesus.

Once you start wanting to obey (on any level), you're switching teams and working with God, not against him, as he helps you remove your sin. And God, who is rich in mercy, grace, and forgiveness, is also patient. He knows how weak you are. He isn't surprised by your failures. He wants to free you from the sin that entangles you. This is never about being good enough for God or earning his approval. If it were, we'd all be sunk—without the cross this chapter would be as theoretical as driving to the moon. Without grace, we could no more be righteous than my '92 Buick could take me to the Apollo 11 landing site.

The purpose of this chapter isn't to convince you to try harder to be good. Rather, I want to help you recognize that righteousness is one of the best gifts God can give. Holiness isn't an obligation as much as a benefit of following Jesus.

I've been building up to this next chapter, not because it's the most important but because it strikes very close to home. It's time to talk about money and the stuff it buys. What's the radically normal approach to money? Is having less stuff more holy than having more? Did Jesus really tell us to sell our possessions? This next chapter might get interesting—and personal.

12

What About Money?

I had decided to work at Starbucks for many reasons, including my love of coffee, the atmosphere, flexible schedules, and medical insurance for part-time employees. But a good salary was not one of the reasons. Even with tips, I didn't make much more than minimum wage. We talked about having Marilyn get a job, but we decided that having her homeschool Grace and Sarah was more important. We cut our spending back more than we thought possible and trusted God to make up for any shortfalls. Without a doubt, we were poorer than we had ever been. Yet even that was an answer to a prayer I had prayed several months prior.

I'm a penny-pincher. As a preteen, I had a habit of logging every cent I spent. Buying a three-cent Jolly Rancher becomes less appealing when you know you'll have to write it down later. Being that cheap allowed me to graduate from college debt free, but it also meant I talked my wife out of spending five dollars on a "first Christmas" ornament when we were newlyweds. Oops.

Generosity has been a major struggle for me (quite unlike my wife). Yet the more I studied the Bible the more I understood that it was nonnegotiable. After many internal arguments, I chose to believe that obedience would bring joy, and I prayed a fateful prayer: "God, please help me become a man of generosity." In his grace, he answered that prayer by reducing our discretionary income to its lowest point in our married life.

I'm sure there are easier ways to learn generosity, but that's what it took for me. There in the midst of having little, my heart changed, and we learned creative ways to be generous. We gave away some of our possessions to those who needed them. When God blessed us with unexpected gifts, we found ways to share them. Marilyn started buying things from neighborhood kids who were raising money for their school. Strange as it seems, Marilyn and I began to fantasize about winning the lottery so we could give more. I can't point to any singular event that changed everything, but it began by simply believing that obeying God's command to be generous would make me happier.

Feeling Guilty

The fact you're reading this book tells me that you probably want to avoid complacent Christianity. Yet for many Christians the biggest thing holding them back from wholehearted devotion is money. We hear so many sermons and messages about giving more and being more generous, but no one ever says how much more is enough. One of the things that made it hard for me to start down the road of generosity was the fear that God would keep asking for more until I had nothing left. Wasn't that the message of the rich young ruler?

> When Jesus heard this, he said to him, "You still lack one thing. Sell everything you have and give to the poor, and you will have treasure in heaven. Then come, follow me."

> When he heard this, he became very sad, because he was very wealthy (Luke 18:22-23).

Is this the pinnacle of obedience? Does anything less amount to complacent Christianity? You can see why I was reluctant to start giving. Giving nothing or even a clean 10 percent seemed safer than wandering down that path.

Something else bothered me. If "sell everything you have and give it away" was the target, why didn't anyone do it? No one had an answer for me. The only response I received was that we should be willing to give everything up if God asked. That seemed to be a cop-out. How convenient that almost no one hears him ask. But my prayers remained shallow for fear that he would ask *me*.

Can you relate? Have you ever felt guilty for buying a new car? Maybe you've felt unspiritual for going on a nice vacation instead of giving the money to the poor. I read a quote from a recent book that asked, "How can we hold in one hand the truth that Jesus loves the poor, the widow, and the orphan, yet hold in our other hand the tickets to our Disney vacation?" That sounds biblical, but is it? Maybe all these questions can be summed up this way: Is spending money on ourselves inherently less holy than giving it away?

> Is spending money on ourselves less holy than giving it away?

Complacent Spending

Not long ago, when my family and I were wandering around an outlet mall looking for some deals, I got a glimpse of the other side of the story. We walked from store to store seeing $250 jeans on clearance for $175 and watching people stand in line for the privilege of shopping for the newest perfume. I had to pull my daughters out of a store that was intent on making them look five years older. I saw with clarity the unrestrained materialism and the overwhelming sense of discontent these stores bred. I muttered to my wife, "How many of these places would go out of business if people were actually content with their lives?"

I believe we're being obsessive when we think God wants everyone to live on as little as possible and give the rest away. But I also believe we're being complacent when we spend our lives accumulating more money and more stuff. We're being complacent when we give away only what's left over and teach our kids (through example) that life really does consist in the abundance of our possessions (in contrast to Luke 12:15). As I walked around that outlet mall, I half wanted to condemn the whole thing and pray down fire from heaven to consume that market of Babylon.[1] Our overindulgence is killing our bodies through gluttony, killing our souls through distraction, and killing our planet through overconsumption.

If I had to choose between the obsessive extreme of giving everything away and the complacent extreme of taking as much as I can, I think obsessiveness would be healthier for everyone concerned. But are those the only choices? Is it a sin to buy nice things? Does God have anything to say about buying $175 jeans? Would Jesus take his nieces and nephews to Disneyland?

Money Is Complicated

When it comes to talking about money and possessions, the Bible is complicated. Understandably so—we have a very complicated relationship with the stuff of earth. On one hand, the Bible treats material blessings as gifts from God. In fact, the Bible has far more positive things to say about money than negative. Here's one example among many: "Humility is the fear of the LORD; its wages are riches and honor and life" (Proverbs 22:4).

This verse and others like it are often misused to promote an unbiblical prosperity gospel. (This is a teaching that says God's will is for every Christian to be blessed financially and physically. If you are sick or poor, it says, the reason must be because of some sin or lack of faith on your part). But that doesn't mean we should ignore them—it's all the more reason to teach what they actually mean. Verses like this one teach that money, possessions, and health are some of the earthly joys that God graciously grants and they are frequently rewards for righteousness. *Some* and *frequently* are key words—perhaps the greatest error of the prosperity gospel is assuming that God's blessings are always earthly. In fact, he must occasionally remove earthly blessings in order to grant us spiritual ones (as my time at Starbucks taught me).

On the other hand, I've heard pastors dismiss all such passages, contending that they're all in the Old Testament. They're not. The New Testament also has good things to say about material success.[2] More important, Jesus and the apostles were not so dismissive of the Old Testament. It's not as if God thought material blessings were good things in the Old Testament but realized in the New Testament that they were bad. Instead, the New builds on the Old, adding a greater emphasis on the spiritual danger of accumulating possessions.[3]

The Bible is filled with such warnings. The Old Testament prophets frequently denounced the ungodly rich, especially those who gained their wealth through oppression and injustice.[4] Jesus did the same, as did James.[5] The apostle Paul writes this warning:

> Those who want to get rich fall into temptation and a trap and into many foolish and harmful desires that plunge people into ruin and destruction. For the love of money is a root of all kinds of evil. Some people, eager for money, have wandered from the faith and pierced themselves with many griefs (1 Timothy 6:9-10).

The problem isn't with having money but with wanting to get rich, loving money, being eager for it, and getting it any way you can. Proverbs is filled with similar warnings, including the prayer "give me neither poverty nor riches."[6] Even warning people against being "eager for money" is too radical for many of us. It seems so anti-American.[7]

So what about the rich young ruler? Yes, Jesus clearly tells this man to sell everything. But earlier, when he talks to his disciples, Jesus says, "Sell your possessions." Do you see the difference? Jesus says "everything" to one but not to the others.[8] Am I making too big of a deal of one missing word? In Luke 22:36 the disciples still owned wallets, suitcases, and coats. Either they had disobeyed Jesus's command in 12:33 or they understood that Jesus had told them to sell some of their stuff and keep some.

But what about this passage? "Those of you who do not give up everything you have cannot be my disciples" (Luke 14:33).

Take a look at the context. Jesus said this shortly after telling his disciples to hate their parents, siblings, spouse, and children, so we know he is using some hyperbole here. Also, Jesus doesn't tell them to sell everything, but to give it up. The English Standard Version uses the word *renounce*. Jesus's point is that neither our family nor our possessions should get in the way of following him wholeheartedly.

So here's the good news. Selling everything and giving it to the poor isn't the gold standard for followers of Jesus. But don't get too excited. Jesus tells us to do something that's even harder, because it's not easily dismissed as hyperbole. Jesus actually expects you and me to give away some of our stuff and learn to keep our treasure in heaven instead of on earth. We'll get to that shortly.

Dangerous Tools

Perhaps the best anniversary gift Marilyn has given me was a really sharp kitchen knife. Cooking is just more fun with a good knife. I can slice a tomato paper thin and dice an onion with ease. However, it works equally well on fingers. Luckily, I still have all ten. Actually, it's not luck. I treat that knife with great caution. I watched videos on safe knife-handling technique, I never leave it in the sink, and I don't let Grace and Sarah use it.

God gives us only as much money as we can safely handle—which for some of us is the equivalent of a plastic butter knife.

Money (and the stuff it buys) is like a knife. Having more possessions is like having an even sharper knife. Having lots of money can be fun and can help you do good things, but it's also dangerous. The Bible has much to say about using money carefully because God doesn't want us to cut anything off. I'm inclined to think that God gives us only as much money as we can safely handle—which for some of us is the equivalent of a plastic butter knife.

God's commands and cautions about money and possessions are always for our own good. Obedience protects us from the dangers of money. Why are money and possession so dangerous? I can think of at least two reasons.

Money as Master

First, money tends to master us. Possessions quickly possess us. We end up serving the things that were meant to serve us. For instance, being a home owner is nice, but having a house means taking care of a house. Marilyn and I tried to sell our house so we could be free from the financial burdens that came with ownership. Have you ever thought about how much of your time and money is spent taking care of your stuff?

Stuff isn't necessarily bad, but it sure is needy! Our abundance of possessions naturally steals time and energy away from God, family, friends, and church. And unless we're careful, it will displace God as our master. "No one can serve two masters. Either you will hate the one and love the other, or you will be devoted to the one and despise the other. You cannot serve both God and money" (Matthew 6:24).

Why do money and possessions master us so easily? I think it's because we tend to use them for the wrong jobs. My kitchen knife works great on tomatoes, but if I ever tried to use it to trim my fingernails, I might end up losing a fingertip. We want money to take care of us—to provide security for the future, give us our identity, and make us happy. We want clothes to make us feel valuable and toys to protect us from relationships and vulnerability. Money and possessions can't do those things because they weren't meant to. Our security comes from God.

> Unless the LORD builds the house,
>   the builders labor in vain.
> Unless the LORD watches over the city,
>   the guards stand watch in vain.
> In vain you rise early
>   and stay up late,
> toiling for food to eat—
>   for he grants sleep to those he loves (Psalm 127:1-2).

You are a child of God—that's your identity. Without God, all the pleasures of this life are vain distractions (as the Teacher of Ecclesiastes discovered). With God, however, they may bring real joy. When we look to God to provide what only he can provide, our money and possessions become tools in his hands.

Distraction

The second reason money and possessions are so dangerous is that they are temporary things that easily distract us from eternal things. Look at the bigger quote about selling our possessions.

> Sell your possessions and give to the poor. Provide purses for yourselves that will not wear out, a treasure in heaven that will never fail, where no thief comes near and no moth destroys. For where your treasure is, there your heart will be also (Luke 12:33-24).

Years ago I had a little Chevy Metro that desperately needed a front-end alignment. I had to apply constant pressure to the right just to drive straight (I should have gotten it fixed, but it was cheaper to keep buying spare tires from the junkyard).

Our possessions are like that. They naturally pull our attention, focus, and allegiance away from spiritual things—not because they're bad but because they're so tangible. Like driving my Metro, we must apply constant pressure just to keep going straight. The moment we start mindlessly going with the flow, our treasure shifts from heaven to earth.

Safe Practices

So how do we keep ourselves from being mastered and distracted by our money and possessions? Frankly, an obsessive vow of poverty would be simpler—not more fun or holier, but simpler. It reminds me of how many good Christian teenage boys struggle with lust. There's one option my youth pastor never suggested—total emasculation. That would do the trick, but it's clearly not the right answer. Like sex, possessions are good gifts that God has given us and wants us to enjoy in the right way. God's plan isn't to remove desire, but to direct it to the right purpose. So how do we enjoy earthly possessions without being possessed by them? Here are three

If you're not content with what you currently have, you'll never be content.

practices that have been helpful to me, all of which are found in the passages we've already looked at.

Practice Contentment

First, prior to warning against the pursuit of wealth, Paul says this: "But godliness with contentment is great gain. For we brought nothing into the world, and we can take nothing out of it. But if we have food and clothing, we will be content with that" (1 Timothy 6:6-8).

The secret is practicing contentment. If I have the basics covered, I'll be content. Paul was a traveling missionary, so he needed a little less than I do as a husband and father of two, but we all know about the gap between what we need and what we want. Here are some of my own helpful reminders.

- My car doesn't have air conditioning, but it runs, so I am content.

- My house doesn't have a view, but it shelters me, so I am content.

- I'm not eating gourmet, but I am eating, so I am content.

- My clothes are last year's style, but they fit, so I am content.

Destitution and absolute poverty are evidence of a world broken by sin. God never intended people to live with their basic needs unmet. But once our basic needs are taken care of, contentment is possible. In fact, if you aren't content with that, you never will be. Let me repeat that—if you're not content with what you currently have, you'll never be content. You'll always want just a little more. A small raise, a newer car, a bigger wardrobe. Nothing will be enough without contentment. Contentment brings freedom and joy, but greed and ingratitude bring slavery and misery.

Does that mean that Christians are allowed to have only the basics and then must give everything away after that? That's not what Paul said. In Philippians 4:12 he says that he's also content in plenty. But we must understand that anything beyond the basics is the icing on the cake and appreciate it as such.

Practice Simplicity

The second thing that protects us from the dangers of money is practicing simplicity. This comes from what Jesus said about selling some of your possessions. Why didn't he say, "Give your possessions to the poor"? Because there are two separate commands here—sell stuff and give to the poor. Jesus seems to be commanding us to get rid of some, but not all, of our stuff.

The very act of getting rid of stuff frees our souls. When we tried to sell our house, our Realtor showed us how to stage it, which largely meant stashing half of our stuff in the garage. When it didn't sell and we took it off the market, we realized how much happier we were with that much less stuff. Grace and Sarah didn't even miss all the extra toys. Rather than moving all of it back out of the garage, we decided to get rid of most of it. Some we sold, some we gave away, and some we threw away.

> Generosity is the best of both worlds—it focuses our attention more on heaven while allowing us to enjoy earth more.

Practicing simplicity isn't a matter of giving something up, but of gaining joy. Maybe this is one of those "you have to try it to believe it" things, but I seriously love having less stuff. At the same time, I know that some people can also become obsessive and legalistic about simplicity. Extreme simplicity isn't necessarily godlier than hoarding.

Practice Generosity

Practicing generosity not only protects us from the dangers of money but also brings more joy than we can imagine. Understand, generosity isn't optional for believers. It's commanded in various forms in almost every book of the Bible. It's a fundamental principle of life—we are blessed to be a blessing, just as Abraham was. God told him, "I will make you into a great nation, and I will bless you; I will make your name great, and you will be a blessing" (Genesis 12:2).

Generosity is the best of both worlds—it focuses our attention more on heaven while allowing us to enjoy earth more. Whenever God gives something to us, he expects us to give it to others in turn. He gives us life, and we share it with others. He gives us grace and salvation, and we share them. He gives us money and possessions, and we share those too. Paul believed this. "You will be enriched in every way so that you can be generous on every occasion, and through us your generosity will result in thanksgiving to God" (2 Corinthians 9:11).

To Whom Much Is Given

During the summer, Marilyn likes to have Otter Pops or similar popsicles on hand. Because they're so cheap, we can freely give them to neighbor kids without decimating the food budget. Usually we hand them to Grace and Sarah and ask them to give them to the other kids. How do you think we'd feel if we found Sarah hiding in a corner, covered in multicolored stains and holding six empty Otter Pop containers? I'm guessing that's how God feels when we're stingy with what he gives us to share.

I've witnessed a certain silliness among obsessive Christians. They try to make the rest of us feel bad for our prosperity as Western Christians while almost glamorizing (or at least spiritualizing) the suffering of poorer nations. We have been given much—not in order to feel guilty, and not so we can live excessively. Rather, we have been entrusted with much so we can bless others. "From everyone who has been given much, much will be demanded; and from the one who has been entrusted with much, much more will be asked" (Luke 12:48).

Again, generosity isn't optional. Don't gloss over the intensity of this statement.

> If anyone has material possessions and sees a brother or sister in need but has no pity on them, how can the love of God be in that person? Dear children, let us not love with words or speech but with actions and in truth (1 John 3:17-18).

God could provide for every need, feed every person, meet every church budget, and fully support every missionary without our cooperation. Instead he chooses to meet all of these needs through us. This isn't efficient, but it gives us the honor and joy of partnering with him.

The downside is that our failure to embrace this honor means that people go hungry, churches shut down, and the gospel goes unpreached.

I wrote this chapter after "Happy Holiness" because I want to motivate you with joy, not guilt. I believe from personal experience that obeying God's command to be generous will bring you more happiness, not less. A friend of mine went to Cancún and decided to give exceedingly generous tips to the underpaid staff instead of buying a lot of souvenirs. He has no doubt that he enjoyed himself more than those who spent all their money on themselves.

How Much Is Enough?

How can you know when you have given enough? At what point can you enjoy what you have without guilt? Just as you can never practice the spiritual disciplines enough, you can never give enough. If all Christians were to give every cent they had, they couldn't solve all the world's problems. Natural disasters, crime, and injustice would still impoverish some, and foolish living would impoverish others. The poor we will always have with us.[9] But if it weren't for grace, we would have to be obsessively generous in an attempt to do it all and keep God happy. Instead, we get to gratefully partner with him and allow him to do what we cannot.

Even still, how do we know if we're doing our part? The last time I asked how much is enough (chapter 10), I used the image of balancing on a post. Now I want to compare it to playing on a football field. Generosity isn't as simple as "Give this percentage to God and the rest is yours." It's all God's. Rather, consider these two principles that mark either end of the football field.

On one end is the principle of being sacrificial but not suicidal in your giving. In 2 Corinthians, Paul mentions that the Macedonian churches gave "as much as they were able, and even beyond their ability." Yet he also said, "Our desire is not that others might be relieved while you are hard pressed."[10]

On the other end of the field is enjoying what you have while sharing freely. We see this in the example of the virtuous woman of Proverbs 31.

She opens her arms to the poor
  and extends her hands to the needy.
When it snows, she has no fear for her household;
  for all of them are clothed in scarlet.
She makes coverings for her bed;
  she is clothed in fine linen and purple
      (Proverbs 31:20-22).

She's generous, opening her arms to the poor. Yet her hard work affords her many luxuries—fine linens, purple clothing, and even imported food (verse 14). As you may already know, purple dye was insanely expensive in ancient days. According to some accounts, purple clothes could cost their weight in gold. Compared to that, $175 jeans are a bargain! I don't think the Proverbs 31 woman would have had any problem holding God's love for the poor in one hand and her family's Disneyland tickets in the other.

Being radically normal means moving up and down this field, freed from guilt and filled with joyful generosity. At times (particularly when you're getting too attached to your stuff), God will call you to be more sacrificial. At other times he will allow you to enjoy the fruits of your labor and the joys of this life.

Notice what isn't on the field—having but not sharing, accumulating excessive wealth, spending everything on yourself and your family. From beginning to end, the entire scope of Scripture agrees that stinginess is a sin. It's as unacceptable as lying or stealing. Indeed, it's stealing from God.

"Will a mere mortal rob God? Yet you rob me. "

But you ask, 'How are we robbing you?' "

In tithes and offerings. You are under a curse—your whole nation—because you are robbing me. Bring the whole tithe into the storehouse, that there may be food in my house. Test me in this," says the Lord Almighty, "and see if I will not throw open the floodgates of heaven and pour out so much blessing that there will not be room enough to store it (Malachi 3:8-10).

The point here isn't that tithing is a shrewd investment scheme, but that stinginess is robbing from God and has consequences. It's also a promise that God will take care of you in your obedience. Even as my family became more generous with less resources, we never lacked for what we needed.

A Call to Generosity

Let me end this section with these pastoral exhortations.

Don't wait until you have more resources to start being generous because you'll never feel as if you have enough. I don't want God to cut your income as much as he did mine in order for you to learn generosity. Pray for God to help you see the joy in giving and then obey with whatever you have.

Give intentionally to key areas that need support, including your church, missions, and nonprofits that you believe in—especially ones that help the poor and disadvantaged.

Give spontaneously. Make sure you have a little extra room in your budget and look for opportunities to bless people. (This can provide some of the biggest thrills of giving.)

As you learn to be content, intentionally build more room for generosity into your budget. I like this quote from Randy Alcorn: "God prospers me not to raise my standard of living, but to raise my standard of giving." When you get a raise, don't simply spend all of it on yourself. Daydream about how much fun you'd have being more generous. Start living those dreams now. Don't wait until you have more money.

Finally, if you have children, never forget how much you're teaching them by example about money and generosity. I don't need to tell you how happy I was when Grace described what she'd do if she were a real princess. "First I'd give money to people who don't have any. Then I'd get a pony."

The minute we get serious about obedience, we are in danger of thinking we're better than Christians who don't appear to be following suit. The church seems to spend most of its time bouncing between legalism and worldliness. In reality, both of those options are lazy ways out. Learning to consistently live between legalism and worldliness is much harder, but it's also much more fun.

13

Between Legalism and Worldliness, Part 1

About two months after I began at Starbucks, I was working in the drive-through when a customer pulled up to my window with an open Budweiser can in his lap. Maybe that's kosher in your neck of the woods, but drinking and driving is frowned upon in Washington State.

"What's that?" I asked sharply.

"Uhh…" the driver responded, looking guilty.

"Is that beer?" I asked again.

"It's from yesterday."

"I don't care if it's from last week. You can't have an open can of beer in your car."

"Really, it's fine."

"Really, it's not. I'm not letting you drive away with that." He just stared at me and hung on to his beer, so I snapped into daddy mode. "Gimmie the beer," I commanded. He blinked in disbelief. I repeated myself slowly. "Give me the beer, or I'll call the cops." Looking a little dazed, he slowly handed me the half-empty can.

As he drove off and I emptied the beer down the sink, my manager was laughing so hard he struggled to talk to me. "Did you really just confiscate someone's beer?" he finally asked.

"Yeah. I didn't know what else to do."

"You were scary. I would have given you my beer."

That incident earned me a place in my local Starbucks's lore, but not everyone was amused. One partner accused me of sticking my nose into other people's business, of being legalistic, judgmental, and the like.

In my attempt to avoid legalism, was I skirting the edge of worldliness and leading my church to do the same?

That stung. I've worked hard to avoid legalism, and I hate to be accused of it.

Other people think I work too hard to avoid legalism. I once had an idealistic young man accuse me of pastoring a worldly church and saying we didn't really care about holiness. I wanted to dismiss him as an obsessive Christian (which may or may not have been true), but I had to ask myself if his words held any truth. In my attempt to avoid legalism, was I skirting the edge of worldliness and leading my church to do the same?

Legalism and worldliness are other ways to describe the two cliffs I described in chapter 2, the cliffs of self-righteousness and destructive sin. Many in my generation are so haunted by the legalism of past generations that they plow unthinkingly into the opposite extreme. But I'm convinced that the life God desires and that brings the greatest joy can be found only by avoiding both cliffs. In the next two chapters, we'll take a look at how to avoid the extremes of legalism and worldliness.

The Danger of Safety

Wholeheartedly pursing obedience isn't legalism—it's happy holiness. We fall off the cliff of legalism when we think our status with God depends on how well we obey. We can also fall off when we live our lives by a list of rules that exceed those in the Bible and expect others to do the same. This second kind of legalism is what Jesus was talking about when he rebuked the Pharisees.

> The Pharisees and teachers of the law asked Jesus, "Why don't your disciples live according to the tradition of the elders instead of eating their food with defiled hands?"

He replied, "Isaiah was right when he prophesied about you hypocrites; as it's written:

> "'These people honor me with their lips,
>   but their hearts are far from me.
> They worship me in vain;
>   their teachings are merely human rules.'

"You have let go of the commands of God and are holding on to human traditions" (Mark 7:5-8).

By Jesus's day, Jewish leaders had expanded the commands of God and added traditions designed to prevent even the slightest chance of breaking any given command. For instance, the Torah says, "Do not cook a young goat in its mother's milk" (Exodus 23:19). The ancient rabbis expanded the rule to prohibit eating any meat with any dairy products. This was meant to create a fence around the Law and prevent any possibility of an infraction. Some Jews expand this even further by not using the same utensils for both. A Christian friend of mine worked on an Israeli kibbutz (a farming collective), and she caused a huge fiasco when she accidently washed the dishes used for meat in the sink used for milk. A rabbi from Jerusalem had to oversee the cleansing of the dishes and sink. (I wonder if that got her out of kitchen duty.)

The problem is that fences provide only the illusion of safety.

The human traditions that Jews have added to God's commands don't concern me as much as the traditions that Christians continue to add today. Obsessive Christianity likes to create all sorts of extrabiblical rules to keep us extra-safe.

- The Bible tells us to save sex for marriage, so couples shouldn't kiss until their wedding day.
- Drunkenness is forbidden, so Christians shouldn't drink any alcohol.
- The Bible commands modesty, so Christians should never wear a two-piece bathing suit.

- The Bible says to guard our hearts, so Christians shouldn't watch R-rated movies.

- The Bible says our bodies are temples of the Holy Spirit, so Christians shouldn't smoke (though eating fast food is fine).

These are not necessarily bad rules, but they're not in the Bible. Rather, these rules are our fences—human traditions added to the commands of God in order to keep us from getting too near the edge of the cliff. Sometimes they're legitimatized with the exhortation to avoid even the appearance of evil.[1] So what's the problem with these fences? Even if they are just human traditions, aren't they there to keep us safe? Better safe than sorry!

The problem is that fences provide only the illusion of safety.

First, fences aren't nearly as strong as they look. The couple that uses "no kissing until marriage" to keep them from premarital sex may discover they can skip first base and head straight for home pretty easily.

Second, fences tend to focus on external, observable behavior without examining internal attitudes and motives. In many churches, a Sunday school teacher could get away with being self-righteous, arrogant, and quarrelsome as long as the kids never see her using chew. In the words of a classic song of my youth, "Hide the Beer, the Pastor's Here"...

> And the hate in your heart you're hiding well
> But the booze on your breath is easy to smell

Finally, fences only provide an illusion of safety because there are two cliffs, not one. Fences can help protect you from getting too close to the cliff of destructive sins, but in the process they push you closer to the cliff of legalism. If you choose to be really strict about dress, entertainment, or beverage choices, you may be safer from falling into destructive sins. The teetotaler is in no danger of drunk driving. But at the same time you increase your risk of legalism, self-righteousness, self-reliance, pride, and joylessness.

The Proper Use of Fences

Does that mean fences are bad? Not necessarily. I was closing one night at Starbucks with the shift manager and an unmarried female barista. As we were getting ready to leave, the barista said, "Josh, do you mind giving me a ride tonight?" The request put me in an awkward position because I have a personal policy of avoiding being alone with any woman I'm not related to, even for a short car ride.

Unfortunately, she had more or less planned on me giving her a ride, and I was not about to let her walk home in the dark. I called my wife and let her know I was making an exception to the rule, and then I tactfully explained to my friend that this was a one-time occurrence. I also made a point of talking to my wife on my phone for most of the ride. I could tell my coworker was completely baffled (and annoyed) by this policy of mine, but I didn't care. I put this fence in place because I've watched a lot of pastors fall into sexual immorality and seen the devastation it's wreaked on their families and congregations.

The problem isn't with fences themselves. Even the apostle Paul permitted their use. "I am convinced, being fully persuaded in the Lord Jesus, that nothing is unclean in itself. But if anyone regards something as unclean, then for that person it is unclean" (Romans 14:14).

The problem comes when we try to build fences for other people. Believing that all Christians should obey God's commands isn't legalism, but believing they should observe the extra rules you've added for yourself is. Fences can be invaluable tools. The trick is using them to protect yourself from one cliff without being pushed toward the other. Here are two principles that have helped me do that.

First, understand that your fences are for you. They're based on your own situation, weaknesses, and personal history. The recovering alcoholic probably should not go into a bar. The guy who struggles with lust may not even be able to watch a PG movie. Each of us is strong in some areas and weak in others, which is why we should usually stick to building our own fences. [2]

Second, don't be proud of your fences or lack of them. One of the great dangers of fences is thinking they make you a better Christian.

In Romans 14–15, Paul was basically dealing with an issue of fences regarding what Christians were allowed to eat.

> The one who eats everything must not treat with contempt the one who does not, and the one who does not eat everything must not judge the one who does, for God has accepted them. Who are you to judge someone else's servant? To their own master, servants stand or fall. And they will stand, for the Lord is able to make them stand (Romans 14:3-4).

In essence, Paul says that the person without fences must not look down on or feel superior to the Christian with fences. I've known many Christians who have felt patronized by other Christians for their avoidance of movies, alcohol, or other such things. On the other hand, Christians with certain fences must not judge the liberties of Christians who don't need them. I've also heard Christians with more fences say (in essence), "If you really cared about holiness, you'd have this fence as well."

Romans 14 provides the best antidote to legalism—keep your eyes on Jesus. "To their own master, servants stand or fall." Stop comparing yourself to other Christians and start focusing on your relationship with him. It's all about leaning into Jesus, being empowered by his Spirit, and accepting his forgiveness when you fail. In a word, it's all about grace.

On the other side of legalism is the danger of worldliness. Do you get nervous whenever you hear a sermon on hating the world? I know I do. I'm always afraid that it will end with a demand that we burn all of our secular music and throw away our TVs. Yet worldliness is a real problem, and the Bible calls us to hate the world. What does that actually mean?

14

Between Legalism and Worldliness, Part 2

Another time when I was working in the drive-through, I heard a familiar voice ordering a Frappuccino over my wireless headset. I checked the video monitor to make sure it was my friend and then said, "Are you sure about that? Those have a lot of calories." The other partners looked at me with shock, but I continued, "At least order it without whipped cream."

Over the headset, we heard the customer slowly respond, "No, I really want the whipped cream on that."

My friend pulled up to the window looking a little offended, but when he saw me standing there with a big grin on my face, he burst out laughing. That was so much fun, I pulled similar stunts on other friends.

The headsets were not just used for business, of course. Whenever things slowed down, the partners would crack jokes, tease each other, and talk about whatever. I worked with a lot of non-Christians, so the conversation wasn't always squeaky clean. Profanity doesn't bother me much, but the gossip and crude remarks would grate on me after a while. I had to keep the headset on, so I was forced to hear many conversations I would have been happier without.

What I heard may be mild compared to what you have to deal with on a daily basis, but I struggled with knowing how to respond. Would I sound judgmental if I asked them to cut back on the gossip? Would I weaken my witness by laughing at a hilarious but crude joke? How clean did my jokes have to be? I don't think any of us want to be thought of as self-righteous Christians who can't enjoy a good joke, but when are we in danger of loving the world?

Loving the World

My Grams (Grandma Kelley) grew up in a conservative Pentecostal denomination in the 1930s. She told me she was almost kicked out of her Bible club because she went to a movie theater. The issue wasn't the movie she watched—simply going to the cinema was taboo. If I remember correctly, wearing lipstick may have also been involved. Is it any surprise that to me, "hating the world" has become synonymous with not going to the movies or wearing lipstick? (Not that I wear lipstick.)

These days, I hear a lot of sermons about legalism but very few about worldliness. I've shied away from preaching about worldliness for fear of appearing legalistic. Yet I'm learning that the best reaction to one extreme isn't the other extreme—it's balance. Furthermore, if

If we aren't careful, we can end up hating the wrong world.

we believe that God's commands are for our joy, we can approach what he says about worldliness with the expectation that it will lead us to more joy, not less.

Worldliness is a real thing, and the Bible has strong things to say about it. "You adulterous people, don't you know that friendship with the world means enmity against God? Therefore, anyone who chooses to be a friend of the world becomes an enemy of God" (James 4:4).

"Adulterous people" brings to mind the Old Testament picture of God as a righteously jealous husband. Both the Old and New Testaments tell us that God has no interest in an open relationship. We have to choose between God and the world. He will not share us with another lover.

Clearly, we are supposed to hate the world, but problems arise when we don't clarify exactly what we mean by *the world*. We need to take a closer look at what this word means because if we aren't careful, we can end up hating the wrong world.

Just yesterday I listened to a well-known pastor give a stern admonition to "culture-embracing evangelicals" based on 2 Timothy 4:10: "Demas, because he loved this world, has deserted me." This pastor warned against falling in love with the things of the world and abandoning Jesus. His message was either a biblical call away from complacent Christianity or an unbiblical call to obsessive Christianity, but I'm not sure which. Why not? Because he wasn't careful to define which world he was talking about.

The Bible frequently talks about the world (Greek, *kosmos*), but it doesn't mean the same thing each time. Did your pastor ever tell you Greek is a wonderfully precise language? That's a myth we perpetuate to make our sermons sound more authoritative. Greek can be every bit as ambiguous as English, if not more so. In both Greek and English, many words do double or triple duty. Think of all the different meanings for the word *run*: to jog, to operate, to function, to campaign...or even a place you keep chickens.

Likewise, the Bible uses *the world* in several different ways. It means things like creation, the earth, culture, the things of this life (like food and clothing), and people. Or it can mean the realm that is ruled by Satan and is hostile to God.[1] That is why the Bible can say, "For God so loved the world" (John 3:16) and yet commands us, "Do not love the world or anything in the world" (1 John 2:15).

How are we supposed to know which world a Bible verse is referring to? As with English, the answer is usually obvious from the context.

> Do not love the world or anything in the world. If anyone loves the world, love for the Father is not in them. For everything in the world—the lust of the flesh, the lust of

the eyes, and the pride of life—comes not from the Father
but from the world (1 John 2:15-16).

John isn't talking about hating the culture, cheeseburgers, music,
jokes, or clothes. "Everything in the world" means the "lust of the flesh"
and all that stuff. We are warned not to get too attached to the things
of this life because "this world in its present form is passing away"
(1 Corinthians 7:31), but those things are not in any sense bad.[2] God
will gladly give you these things (in the right
times and the right ways) as gifts from a loving
Father. But he will not share your loyalty and
fidelity with false gods and corrupt desires that
compete with him.

Learning to enjoy earthly things but hate worldliness is central to being radically normal.

Worldliness is giving your heart to beliefs, pri-
orities, and spiritual powers that are opposed to
God. (For the sake of clarity, I will use the words
worldly and *worldliness* to refer only to that which opposes God.) So
long as we live on this planet, surrounded by this worldliness, we will
feel a constant tug on our souls to be unfaithful to our Savior, to sleep
with the enemy, as it were. Being faithful to him requires constant
attention and help from the Spirit.

The point is that every time we see the word *world* in the Bible, we
must think about which meaning the author is using. Just because
something is earthly doesn't mean it's worldly. Learning to enjoy
earthly things but hate worldliness is central to being radically normal.
Obsessive Christianity avoids many earthly things for fear of worldliness. Complacent Christianity loves both earthly and worldly things
without discerning which is which.

Finding the Good in the Bad

Let's talk about how to distinguish between earthly and worldly
things. In chapter 13 I mentioned avoiding even the appearance of evil.
That might sound a little obsessive, but isn't it the pinnacle of holiness? Doesn't radical obedience include avoiding not only sin but also
things that look like sin? The funny thing about that expression is that

it doesn't exist in any of the modern versions because it's a poor trans-lation.[3] Here's a better translation: "Do not quench the Spirit. Do not treat prophecies with contempt but test them all; hold on to what is good, reject every kind of evil" (1 Thessalonians 5:19-22).

There's a big difference between rejecting every kind of evil and rejecting anything that looks evil to anyone. When you think about it, Jesus did a lot of things that appeared sinful to the Pharisees (includ-ing healing on the Sabbath and hanging out with sinners), but he never sinned.

Paul demonstrates a moderate approach here—don't accept every-thing, but don't reject everything either. Rather, test and carefully examine it. Paul is specifically talking about prophecy, but this prin-ciple applies to nearly every area of life. We use the expression "Don't throw out the baby with the bathwater" to say much the same thing. Biblical Christianity assumes that everything is good unless God says it's bad. "For everything God created is good, and nothing is to be rejected if it is received with thanksgiving, because it is consecrated by the word of God and prayer" (1 Timothy 4:4-5).

If it's sin, reject it. If it's not, you may embrace it with prayer and thanksgiving. Of course, it would be far simpler to hold on to the good and reject the evil if everything fit neatly into those categories. Ever since the Fall, sin has contaminated every nook and cranny of this world, so we have to be diligent to test everything. To learn how to do that, let's focus on how we approach one earthly thing that can be extremely worldly—entertainment.

Watch What You Watch

When I was a freshman at Bible college, students were not allowed to have TVs in their dorm rooms, so the TV in the student lounge was pretty popular. One evening, as a bunch of us were watching *The Simp-sons*, an older and wiser senior came in. Right about then, something really funny but irreverent happened, and I laughed really loud. The senior spun around and said, "Would you laugh at that if your pas-tor were here?"

"You don't know my pastor," I thought but didn't say. Instead, I just kind of shrugged, and he stormed away muttering something about worldliness.

Growing up, my family had a TV but no cable. We were stuck with whatever stations our coat-hanger antenna could pick up. Even with the limited selection, my parents had a list of shows we were not allowed to watch, such as *He-Man* and *The Smurfs*. I used to laugh at that list until I had daughters and saw some of the stuff Grace and Sarah's friends watched. I wonder if they'll laugh at me someday because I don't let them watch *Bratz*. I now have more respect for the challenges my parents faced as they tried to protect us from worldliness without being legalistic.

As I mentioned, in my grandparents' day, all movies were considered taboo by many Christians. By the time I was born, G-rated movies were acceptable, but the idea of a Christian watching an R-rated movie was scandalous. Now many pastors routinely use R-rated movies for sermon illustrations. As much as I want to dismiss the archaic "no movies" rules as silly legalism, Philippians 4:8 gives me pause. "Finally, brothers and sisters, whatever is true, whatever is noble, whatever is right, whatever is pure, whatever is lovely, whatever is admirable—if anything is excellent or praiseworthy—think about such things."

I'm hard-pressed to think of any movie that's only pure, noble, and excellent. Is any amount of worldliness like a drop of poison that contaminates an entire glass of milk? Does one sex scene make the whole thing off-limits? Or can one good teaching point excuse any amount of depravity? And where do we find answers to questions like these? Records of the apostles' favorite movies are sketchy at best.

Live theater and sports were the most popular forms of entertainment in Paul's day. Many Jews and Christians avoided these events because of their immorality and brutality. Athletic events were dedicated to pagan gods, and participants competed in the nude. Ancient theater was filled with sex and potty humor. These forms of entertainment presented challenges to ancient Christians similar to the challenges modern entertainment presents for us.

What do you think Paul would say about sports and theaters? He never tells believers to avoid plays or athletic competitions. Instead, he uses more sports analogies than I do and even quotes from a pagan play.[4] If he wanted his readers to completely avoid these events, he could have easily said so. But instead, he looked for things of value in them.

What about Philippians 4:8? Didn't that imply that early Christians should have avoided the theater and sporting events? Actually, that verse is an example of testing everything and holding on to the good. The Greek words Paul uses seem to indicate he was alluding to pagan philosophy.

> In all probability the apostle is here acknowledging that there was much good in pagan life and morality, and he urges his friends...not to be blind to this fact, nor to repudiate it. He asks, rather, that they recognize and incorporate all that is good in natural morality into their own lives, to pay heed to quite simple but solid truths, even if they first learned them from pagan sources. For as Justin Martyr put it a century later, "The truth which men in all lands have rightly spoken belongs to us" (2 Apol. 2.13).[5]

Paul's point in Philippians 4:8 is the opposite of what I used to believe. "Think about such things" doesn't mean "don't look at anything bad."[6] Rather he wants us to follow his example, to learn how to find and meditate on noble and true things, even if we find them in unlikely places.

I'm not saying Christians can watch whatever they want as long as they can find some valuable piece of wisdom hidden in it. Many movies are so filled with worldliness that trying to find the good in them is like wandering through acres of stinging nettle to find one stalk of wheat. Think carefully about what you fill your mind with because it will affect you.

> Above all else, guard your heart,
>   for everything you do flows from it.
> Keep your mouth free of perversity;
>   keep corrupt talk far from your lips (Proverbs 4:23-24).

Now take this biblical principle of testing everything, keeping the good, and rejecting the evil (2 Thessalonians 5:19-22) and apply it to other areas of your life—the TV shows you watch, the music you listen to, the games you play, and the books you read. Can you find noble and true things in them? Do they have any redeeming value? How are they affecting your soul?

I believe legalism is so popular because it's much easier than carefully evaluating what's earthly and what's worldly.

No one can give you a nice, neat list of what you should or shouldn't allow into your heart. A radically normal Christian thoughtfully chooses movies based on content (not their rating) and then wrestles with what's good and what's worldly. That seems much more edifying than mindlessly watching anything on TV as long as the bad words are bleeped out.

One more thought. Think about how much of your time you spend being entertained. I recently overheard a woman who told another that the video she rented was a waste of a dollar and then laughed because... who cares about a dollar? As I see it, she wasted a lot more than a dollar—she wasted two hours of her life. If you and I want to accomplish some of the great stuff I talked about in chapter 5, we just might have to use our time a little more carefully.

The Easy Way Out

Looking back to the previous chapter, I believe legalism is so popular because it's much easier than carefully evaluating what's earthly and what's worldly. Not better or more fun, but easier. By simply following a list someone gives you, you can feel safe and secure. Likewise, worldliness is pretty easy—just plow thoughtlessly into everything the world (in the bad sense) has to offer. It's also a lot of fun...at least until you start suffering the consequences. It's also easier to mock legalistic Christians than to pursue righteousness.

Going to the extremes of legalism or worldliness might be easier, but either will lead you over a cliff—away from God and toward misery.

Legalism will leave you wondering if you're doing enough. Worldliness will isolate you from the Source of joy. Balancing on the narrow path between them and relying on grace isn't easy, but it is good.

So far, I've been writing with the assumption that life is going pretty well (except when we mess it up with sin). But what if things aren't going well? How do radically normal Christians deal with undeserved pain and suffering?

Don't Waste Pain

When I started working at Starbucks, I was very clear to the store manager that my church was my priority. Working Sunday mornings was not an option. Corri, the store manager, was very understanding and flexible, so we never had any scheduling conflicts. For that same reason, I knew I could never go into management. The church had to stay the main thing.

After I learned the ropes and God dealt with my bad attitude, I found myself enjoying my job at Starbucks—perhaps too much. Remaking a bad latte was easier than taking back a sermon that even my mom slept through. Issues at Starbucks stayed at Starbucks, but I carried church problems with me wherever I went.

As frustrations at church made retreating deeper into my second job easier, my resolve not to be a manager weakened. Then one day Corri asked me to consider a promotion. She understood my church would still have to come first, and she was willing to continue working with my schedule. In my own mind, I was able to come up with all sorts of reasons a promotion would be better for the church, so I accepted her offer. Somewhere deep inside, I knew that management couldn't help but pull more of my heart away from the church, but I convinced myself and my leadership team that it wouldn't. So did it?

I never had the opportunity to find out. Not long after offering me the promotion, Corri had to leave our store unexpectedly because of some medical issues. In the disorder that followed, my promotion fell by the wayside.

God works in strange ways. After being offered a promotion and then having it taken away, I found myself becoming less satisfied with my Starbucks job (but for the right reasons). I didn't realize it at the time, but God was preparing me to return to full-time ministry. He was also speaking to me through my daughters.

The hardest part of working at Starbucks was how much time it took away from my family. Every morning as I left for work, Sarah would pull back my coat to see what shirt I was wearing. A black shirt meant I'd be working at Starbucks that night, and she'd give a patently fake cry. She was mostly being silly, but she knew the black shirt meant she wouldn't see me until the next morning. I'd tell her we needed to be thankful for the job, but she kept up the act. I finally had to tell her how sad it made me.

Not long before God brought me back to full-time ministry, someone asked me if I could switch shifts with them. I eagerly agreed because I would get off earlier and be home just in time to put Grace and Sarah to bed. I powered through my last tasks, hoping to gain just a couple more minutes with my girls. When I got home, I walked into a dark, silent house. No daughters rushing down the stairs to hug me, no wife greeting me. I trudged upstairs to find everyone already asleep in bed, worn out from a full day without me. As I stood in Grace and Sarah's room, watching them lie there, I lost it. I told God I couldn't do this anymore. I missed my family too much. This was too hard.

That was my darkest day at Starbucks.

Better than Laughter

I now understand what God was doing—he was pushing me out of Starbucks. There was nothing bad about working there. I still don't believe that being a pastor is a higher calling than being a barista, but being a pastor is *my* calling. In an effort to avoid the pain of pastoring a struggling church, I had put my heart where it didn't belong.

A couple of years earlier, during my word study on joy in the Bible, I was really puzzled by one passage.

> It is better to go to the house of mourning
> than to go to the house of feasting,
> for this is the end of all mankind,
> and the living will lay it to heart.
> Sorrow is better than laughter,
> for by sadness of face the heart is made glad.
> The heart of the wise is in the house of mourning,
> but the heart of fools is in the house of mirth
> (Ecclesiastes 7:2-4 ESV).

"Sorrow is better than laughter"? That seemed so out of step with everything else the Bible had to say about joy and happiness. But that dark night in my daughters' room and other experiences like it helped me understand. Some things can be learned only through pain. As I thought about it, I realized that my greatest growth has been the result of suffering, whether caused by my own sin, the sin of others, or seemingly random events.

Trying to skip past pain will ultimately deprive us of more joy down the road.

Like you, I am still in process. Even as I write this I'm on the tail end of a new trial, the greatest challenge I've ever faced in ministry. I never want to go through anything like it again, yet I wouldn't be the person I am without it and wouldn't trade it for anything.

I finally understand what Ecclesiastes is saying. If we insist on trying to be happy and positive all the time, we're being not only delusional but also foolish. Trying to skip past pain will ultimately deprive us of more joy down the road.

Songs to a Heavy Heart

Many years ago, my grandma Andrade passed away unexpectedly. The funeral was a mixture of shock, grief, and anger. At the reception, a pastor tried to comfort some family members by leading a little worship time in the corner. My thoughts toward her were un-pastoral to say the least. All I could think of was this verse in Proverbs: "Like one who takes away a garment on a cold day, or like vinegar poured on a wound, is one who sings songs to a heavy heart" (Proverbs 25:20).

Grandma's death was a painful, awful mess—that was all there was to it that day. Later there would be time for healing, but that was the time for mourning. I say all that to say if you are currently in the midst of suffering and this chapter feels like a song sung to a heavy heart, I am truly sorry. You may decide that it's best to skip it for now. Perhaps some of the books listed in appendix 2 will be helpful.

Let me add that suffering is not simple. Some is good and some is bad. Some is mild and some is crushing. Some is self-inflicted, and some is inflicted on the innocent. Some people have had a reasonably good life, and others have faced great hardships. I don't pretend to have walked through the same pain you have. My goal in this chapter is not to explain why bad things happen—other books address that. I begin with the assumption that God, in his goodness, allows suffering. Then I ask (as strange as it may seem), how can God use this suffering to bring me more joy?

Nothing Wasted

My goal is to help all of us make the best use of our suffering because suffering will come to all of us. The promise I see in Romans 8:28 is that no pain has to be wasted.

> We know that in all things God works for the good of those who love him, who have been called according to his purpose. For those God foreknew he also predestined to be conformed to the image of his Son, that he might be the firstborn among many brothers and sisters. And those he predestined, he also called; those he called, he also justified; those he justified, he also glorified (Romans 8:28-30).

This passage is sometimes misquoted to say that everything is good. That is nonsense. The world is filled with pain, sorrow, and evil. These things are not good. Jesus wept at Lazarus's tomb because he knew death was an evil intrusion on the good world he made (John 11:33-37).[1]

Instead, Romans promises that God can transform these things into something good. I've found a lot of comfort and insight in these words from C.S. Lewis.

> They say of some temporal suffering, "No future bliss can make up for it," not knowing that Heaven, once attained, will work backwards and turn even that agony into a glory. And of some sinful pleasure they say "Let me but have this and I'll take the consequences": little dreaming how damnation will spread back and back into their past and contaminate the pleasure of the sin. Both processes begin even before death. The good man's past begins to change so that his forgiven sins and remembered sorrows take on the quality of Heaven: the bad man's past already confirms his badness and is filled only with dreariness. And that is why, at the end of all things, when the sun rises and the twilight turns to blackness down there, the Blessed will say "We have never lived anywhere except in Heaven," and the Lost, "We were always in Hell." And both will speak truly.[2]

Too often, discussions about Romans 8:29-30 are hijacked by arguments about predestination and free will. I think that misses the point. Paul wrote those words to encourage us—God is writing the story of your life, and he knows how it ends. He knows that your story is not a tragedy. He knows that it has a happy ending. Because of that, you can be assured that every scene will work to this end. He is a master weaver, working both the bright and dark threads together to make an amazing picture. The idea is not that suffering is good, but that God will transform your sufferings into something beautiful if you are in Christ.

He is a master weaver, working both the bright and dark threads together to make an amazing picture.

Growing Pains

When I started at Starbucks, I was given a copy of *Onward* by Howard Schultz, the CEO of Starbucks. One key lesson in the book is that success hides the cracks in the foundation. In their boom period, hundreds of Starbucks stores were losing money, the supply chain was bloated and ineffective, and millions of dollars were being wasted. But no one noticed because they were making so much money. Then the recession hit, and they either had to get healthy or risk being bought off. They finally made the painful decisions they should have made years prior. Could they have made these changes during their success? Theoretically, yes. Practically, no.

You and I can learn some things only when things aren't going well. Next time you're suffering, don't focus on the symptoms. Prayerfully ask if you need to deal with cracks in the foundation. Don't assume your suffering is your fault, but don't assume it isn't. Look for good counsel—and not just from friends who are eager to help you feel better as quickly as possible. Even if your suffering came through no fault of your own, you can learn important lessons.

Unfortunately, we usually short-circuit this process by trying to numb our pain. We take another drink, jump into the next relationship, or turn on the TV. But when we attempt to avoid suffering, we most often prolong it. I've witnessed far too many divorces and have noticed a trend among the spouses who were abandoned. Even if they responded to the divorce as righteously as possible, many of them did very unrighteous and destructive things afterward. Usually they jumped into ill-advised relationships with tragically predictable results. I understand that they were in terrible pain and wanted to stop it, but unfortunately, they only increased it.

The single greatest thing we can learn from suffering is to depend more deeply on God. In my recent trials, I held on to one passage more than any other.

> We do not want you to be uninformed, brothers and sisters, about the troubles we experienced in the province of Asia. We were under great pressure, far beyond our ability

to endure, so that we despaired of life itself. Indeed, we felt
we had received the sentence of death. But this happened
that we might not rely on ourselves but on God, who raises
the dead (2 Corinthians 1:8-9).

In times of suffering, we will either run to God or run from him.
We deal with pain by either depending on his grace or rejecting it and
trying to fix things our own way. I've seen people respond to the same
hardships in opposite ways—some by drawing closer to God and some
by pulling away.

When It Doesn't Work

This leads us to the elephant in the room—can we really trust God?
According to the Torah and the book of Proverbs, we're blessed
because of our righteousness, and we suffer because of our wickedness.
Most of the time, this is how things work. But the book of Job provides
a vital balance—it reminds us that things don't always work that way.

Job is as righteous as any human could possibly be, and God has
blessed him tremendously. Job believes that righteousness equals blessing—until that system stops working. Then for 28 chapters, Job's
friends tell him, "You must have really sinned to be suffering like this."
Job counters, "No, I didn't," and they insist, "Yes, you did." The longer the conversation goes, the more they panic—here stands one man
who could bring the whole system crashing down. If Job can suffer
innocently, so can they.

I once had friends whose child died in a car accident, and some
adherents of the prosperity gospel told them it happened because of
sin in their lives. How could anyone say such a horrible thing to griev-
ing parents? Like Job's friends, they were desperate to reassure themselves that it couldn't happen to them.

Throughout the book, Job keeps demanding that God show up and
explain himself. I'm with Job on this. I want to know why God allows
the innocent to suffer. Just think of all the things God could have said.

- "It wasn't me, it was the devil."

- "Your standard of righteousness is way below mine, so you aren't as innocent as you think."

- "Don't worry, I'm going to give you back double what I took."

- "It was because you didn't have enough faith and feared this would happen."

Instead, when God shows up, he ignores Job's questions and spends the next four chapters asking Job a withering barrage of questions (72 by my count), all of them with one basic point—"I'm God and you're not. You aren't capable of understanding everything."

Is God's answer satisfying? No. Somehow oddly comforting? I think so. I may not be able to understand how or why everything happens, but I trust God. I believe that he is good and that he loves me. And when I have a hard time believing in God's goodness in the light of all the world's suffering, I remember that he became a man and willingly suffered with us and for us. I look to Jesus and realize that I can trust the God who suffers with me.

What Now?

As I see it, complacent Christianity tries to avoid pain at all costs. Then it tries to numb whatever pain gets through even if the anesthetic of choice causes more damage in the long run. On the other hand, obsessive Christianity glamorizes suffering and even seeks it in order to gain a sense of spiritual superiority. Being radically normal means that you accept suffering and allow God to use it for your ultimate joy. I hate pain. I hate it so much that I don't want any of it to go to waste. I want to see God wring the most possible good out of all suffering, even if it's as trivial as a stubbed toe.

I'm not pretending that suffering is fun. But it is unavoidable. So what will you do with it? Helen Keller (who could speak with authority about suffering) said, "We could never learn to be brave and patient if there were only joy in the world." So here is my encouragement. Next time you suffer, spend less time asking "Why me?" and more asking God to transform it into something good.

In addition to everything I've said, I also believe that pain reminds us that this world is not our home. And not just pain—I've noticed a very strange (and unexpected) phenomenon in my life. The more I enjoy this world appropriately, the less it feels like home.

Hungry for Heaven

One day, I was working in the drive-through during the afternoon rush. Normally, I was one of the best partners in drive, but that day I was really struggling to keep up. I kept asking customers to repeat their orders and even struggled to make correct change. The other partners had to pick up the slack, and my shift manager asked me if I was okay. I lied and said I was fine, and then I tried to talk myself down from the rising panic. "It's okay. Just focus. You can do this. It's just coffee. Focus." But it wasn't working. I could feel myself spiraling out of control.

Suddenly I realized what was wrong. Over the headset, I said, "I need someone to slide me out." Someone stepped in, and I headed for the back room.

About a minute later, the manager came back to check on me. "What's wrong?" she asked, looking worried.

"I forgot to take my medicine. I'll be fine in about five minutes," I said.

Did I happen to mention that I was recently diagnosed with attention deficit disorder? It's a very strange thing to discover about yourself at age 37. It's as if ten radio stations are always playing in my head at full volume and I can't choose which one to listen to. At any time, I can tell you the gist of the three conversations behind me, the basic layout of the room, and how many squirrels have run past the window, but I probably won't be able to repeat what you just said to me. Ritalin has been a lifesaver for me. My sermons have improved dramatically, writing a book no longer seemed insurmountable, and I was able to focus at Starbucks. Sure enough, five minutes later, I was back in drive-through and doing fine.

After I was diagnosed, I went online to study ADD. It was like having my life accurately described by perfect strangers. How did I not see this sooner? Then I started reading some posts from support groups for the spouses. I used to think Marilyn's expectations were unreasonable. Isn't it normal for husbands to have a panic attack at the thought of sorting laundry? Or to leave their keys in the front door? Or to routinely ignore their wives because they're so absorbed in a project? I used to joke about being an absentminded professor, not realizing how badly my neglect hurt my wife. My diagnosis was a relief to me ("So *that's* why I am this way!") but upsetting to her ("So you're *always* going to be this way?").

I am a broken person. This side of heaven, there will always be something in my brain that doesn't fire right. But we are all broken people—physically, emotionally, sexually, mentally, spiritually, and relationally. Most of the time, life continues on pretty well, but every now and again something happens that makes us cry out, "How long, O Lord?" As the apostle Paul says, we groan, longing to be clothed with our heavenly bodies, free from pain, brokenness, and sorrow. As much as I enjoy this life, I long for the glorious freedom that awaits me.[1]

Hindrance or Help?

I've talked a lot about earthly joys, from a sunset to a good meal with friends. I've also criticized obsessive Christianity, which says that the closer we get to God, the less the things of this earth should matter. As confident as I am about all this, I started to question myself when I reread this line from the parable of the sower. "The seed that fell among thorns stands for those who hear, but as they go on their way they are choked by life's worries, riches and pleasures, and they do not mature" (Luke 8:14).

Grace and Sarah think it's fun to blow dandelion puffs in our backyard, but all I can see are weeds spreading all over the place. Is that what my book will do, spread weeds of "life's worries, riches, and pleasures?" My greatest fear is that my message could choke out wholehearted devotion to God. Similarly, what about Hebrews 12:1, which tells us to "throw off everything that hinders and the sin that so easily entangles"? Earthly joys may not be sinful, but don't they entangle us and keep us from running the race? The joys of this life have undoubtedly entangled many Christians in a complacent faith.

I took some time to reevaluate my life—had earthly joys pulled me further from God or drawn me closer to him? I thought back to a short vacation I had taken with my family a couple of years ago. We went into a gift shop, and my daughters went to the toys, my wife looked at the decorations, and I went to the books. I thumbed through a history of early missionaries to the Northwest and read about a saint who had spent a lifetime establishing missions, hospitals, and schools and then died at a ripe old age in his sleep. My gut response was, "Lucky stiff. Right now you're experiencing the fullness of God's presence." You have to understand, I wasn't having a bad day—I was having a *great* day. The joy of the day only sharpened my anticipation of seeing Jesus.

The joys of earth can pull us away from God, but for me they are signposts directing me to heaven. They cultivate my deep longing for my Savior. This chapter is the pinnacle of the book to me because it contains the truths that have most deeply impacted me. The more I've learned to properly enjoy earthly things, the more I long for heaven. Because I love this life, eternity in God's presence has gone from a distant hope to tangible reality, like something right in front of me but just out of reach.

Ironically, my least-favorite spiritual discipline has been the most helpful in developing this taste for heaven—fasting.

Fasting Makes Me Hungry

A couple of years ago, I began fasting occasionally as a reluctant response to everything I was learning about joy. "You say obeying God will make you happier," whispered my inner monologue, "but you refuse to fast. So do you really believe it or not?" I managed to ignore myself for a while, but finally I broke down and agreed to an experiment. For a month I would fast from all food one day a week, beginning Sunday evening and ending at dinner the following day (roughly from sundown to sundown). At the end of a month, I'd see if fasting made me happier.

So did fasting make me happier? No. I have continued that experiment on and off for the past couple of years, and I still don't enjoy it. Every Sunday evening I'm annoyed that I can't snack, and I begin to dread the following day's fast. Each week I look for reasons to skip the fast "just this week." Monday mornings (already a low day for most pastors) are especially tough. I can feel the lack of food slowing me down and lowering my mood, so I pray for the Holy Spirit's help. The hunger pains kick in around lunchtime, and I pray to remind myself why I'm doing this. By late afternoon I'm relieved to realize I only have an hour or two left. Then, regardless of what my wife prepares, Monday's dinners always taste really good. Every Tuesday morning, I'm almost overjoyed that I get to eat a bowl of cereal.

It's okay to be hungry. That truth is far more profound than it sounds.

So why do I continue? Because fasting teaches me one of the most important lessons I've ever learned—it's okay to be hungry. That truth is far more profound than it sounds.

Let's take a closer look at what Jesus said about fasting.

> Then John's disciples came and asked him, "How is it that we and the Pharisees fast often, but your disciples do not fast?"
>
> Jesus answered, "How can the guests of the bridegroom mourn while he is with them? The time will come when the bridegroom will be taken from them; then they will fast" (Matthew 9:14-15).

This makes it clear that Jesus expects us to fast, but notice why. It's an act of mourning, lamenting our separation from the bridegroom.

We can't see him now, and we long for the time when we will be together again.

My last semester of college was the longest four months of my life. Three days before classes began, I proposed to Marilyn, and she said yes. The next day, she had to get on a plane and fly from Southern California back to Washington State. I tried to work as many hours as possible to distract myself from the aching loneliness, but that plan backfired. I got a weekend job merchandizing Dreyer's ice cream in nondescript grocery stores in neighborhoods where people couldn't afford Dreyer's. It was a mindless job that gave me hours to think about how much I missed my fiancée. I remember tearing up whenever our song ("My Heart Will Go On") played over a store's intercom. I was so happy when that company folded and I got laid off.

Thinking of that semester helps me understand the apostle Paul's deep yearning to see his Savior.

> For to me, to live is Christ and to die is gain. If I am to go on living in the body, this will mean fruitful labor for me. Yet what shall I choose? I do not know! I am torn between the two: I desire to depart and be with Christ, which is better by far; but it is more necessary for you that I remain in the body (Philippians 1:21-24).

What's your gut reaction to that passage? I don't mean just on a bad day—we all have bad days when escaping this life sounds really good. Do you, like Paul, feel eternal hunger pains gnawing away at you even on the good days? Or does Paul's seeming death wish feel bizarre and irrelevant to your daily life?

Hunger Pains

I was nervous the first time I preached on eternal hunger pains. I was afraid that I'd be the only one who felt the things I was describing and that my sermon would be met with blank stares. Instead, I saw eager, almost ravenous eyes staring back at me as if to say, "You mean I'm not the only one who has felt that?"

I now believe that we all feel that eternal hunger pain far more than we realize. We just don't recognize it because we call it by the wrong names. Maybe you call it emptiness. Maybe you call it restlessness. Or maybe being worn out, "like butter scraped over too much bread" (as Bilbo Baggins put it). It's a feeling that has only increased over the years. Maybe you feel guilty because even on a perfect day, you still don't feel satisfied. Or maybe you call it loneliness. If you've never been married, you may think that marriage cures loneliness, but married people know better.

> I'm convinced that God also put in you a heaven-shaped hole that nothing on earth can satisfy.

Emptiness, restlessness, and loneliness are all descriptions of your eternal hunger pains. They're constant reminders that this world isn't your home, that it's broken and cannot fully satisfy you. You've heard of the God-shaped hole that only he can fill. I'm convinced that God also put in you a heaven-shaped hole that nothing on earth can satisfy. The older you get, the bigger that hole feels.

When you feel this hunger, you can respond in one of two ways.

Something Is Wrong with You

If you believe this lie—that something is wrong with you—you will try to satisfy your hunger pains in different ways. Maybe you've tried ungodly and destructive remedies, such as pornography, sexual immorality, drunkenness, or drugs. Maybe you've tried to fix it with things that aren't sinful, like music, books, food, or relationships. But these are also ineffective—they distract you for a while, but the hunger is still there.

Maybe you think you still feel the hunger because you haven't found the right spiritual program or experience to satisfy it. So you seek longer quiet times, more intense worship experiences, or each new spiritual craze. Even these cannot completely remove the hunger. I've seen Christians respond with shock at the suggestion that spiritual things can't fill the hunger pains, but I've also watched them go from revival to prayer meeting to worship concert in constant search of their next spiritual fix.[2]

Something Is Wrong with This World

Something *is* wrong here, and it cannot be fixed. It was broken at the Fall, and we still suffer the effects of that brokenness. This world isn't your home; you were made for something better. God has filled this world with joys and delights that he fully intends for you to enjoy, but he's also given you hunger pains to remind you how temporary they are.

> Go, eat your food with gladness, and drink your wine with a joyful heart, for God has already approved what you do. Always be clothed in white, and always anoint your head with oil. Enjoy life with your wife, whom you love, all the days of this meaningless life that God has given you under the sun—all your meaningless days. For this is your lot in life and in your toilsome labor under the sun (Ecclesiastes 9:7-9).

"Meaningless" is perhaps better translated as "a vapor"—not bad, but insubstantial and short-lived. Reread that passage. As cynical as it seems, it is a vital reminder because if we look to the vapors of this life to fully satisfy us, they will become the weeds and hindrances that Jesus and the author of Hebrews warn against. But if you enjoy them properly, the joys of this life will draw your heart closer to heaven.

Developing Heavenly Appetites

So how do we enjoy the things of this life properly? Of course, you must begin by using them in God-approved ways, as we discussed in chapter 11, but here are two other things that have helped me tremendously.

Cultivate Hunger

As I said, fasting has taught me that it's okay to be hungry and that this world can never completely satisfy me. About once a week, I'm reminded that in the same way I hunger for food, I continually hunger to be in heaven, face-to-face with my Savior. Fasting helps me live in a continual cycle of enjoying this life and then being reminded that it can never fill me. Rather than numbing, ignoring, and running from your eternal hunger pains, cultivate them, know-

I can't help but wonder if joyless Christians will struggle to embrace the joys of heaven.

ing they are pointing you to something beyond this world. "For they are not the thing itself; they are only the scent of a flower we have not found, the echo of a tune we have not heard, news from a country we have never yet visited."[3] Give fasting a try. Seriously. Barring a medical issue, not eating won't kill you. Keep it attainable by just fasting two meals and snacks—from after dinner one day until dinner the next. When the hunger pains start and you instinctively reach for a treat, ask God to remind you that it's okay to be hungry. Don't be surprised that physical hunger can help you cultivate eternal hunger. We frequently fail to appreciate just how much our bodies affect our spirits, but God doesn't.

Even if you can't or won't fast, the next time you feel that sense of emptiness or longing, don't rush to fill it with something. Take a moment to remember that it's okay to be hungry and ask God to help you cultivate your longing for eternity.

Cultivate Joy

Complacent Christianity numbs hunger pains in its search for joy. Obsessive Christianity cultivates hunger pains to the exclusion of joy. Radically normal Christianity, however, cultivates both hunger pains and joy. I said in the previous chapter that there are some things that we can learn only in pain. My editor, Terry Glaspey, observed that there are also some things that we can learn only in joy. God works both good and bad things "for the good of those who love him."

Here's an interesting thought. Because cultivating earthly joy helps cultivate a taste for eternal joy, I can't help but wonder if joyless Christians will struggle to embrace the joys of heaven. They spent their lives fleeing happiness here, so they might need some time to adjust to pursuing it there. For me, the joy I've found in this life is what makes me long so desperately for the next. As I mentioned earlier, I can't understand heaven, but the stuff of earth gives me glimpses. It's like going to Costco and tasting a little sample of a gourmet food. The sample isn't enough to satisfy, but it lets me know I want more. And I do want more, more than this world could ever provide.

I hope you understand that when I talk about heaven, I primarily mean the complete fullness of joy in God's presence, not the place itself. I want to clarify that because technically speaking, we won't be spending eternity in heaven. That's just one of the many misunderstandings we have about eternity.

This Life Matters

As you can imagine, Starbucks goes through a lot of milk, which means they end up with a lot of empty plastic jugs. My city has made residential recycling easy, but commercial recycling is a bit more complicated. After a little bit of legwork, Corri found a recycling service we could work with. That was the easy part. The hard part was getting all of us to change our routines and start using separate bins for garbage and recyclables. Unfortunately, she never got the chance to do so because of the same medical leave that prevented my promotion.[1] But in light of eternity, how much did a couple thousand milk jugs in a landfill really matter? According to the theology of my youth, Jesus would return soon, and this whole world would be burned up.

Around that same time, I was invited to join the board of directors for Mount Vernon's homeless shelter, the Friendship House. Friendship House is faith based but not strictly Christian—the mission statement talked about God but not Jesus. Also according to the theology of my youth, what was the point of giving people a place for their earthly bodies if we weren't also obsessive about trying to get their souls into heaven?

Maybe the theology of my youth was missing something.

It's All Gonna Burn

I've made no attempts to hide my love of this world in all its breath-taking glory. I've been dumbstruck by stars beyond number and wept under the northern lights. I've taught my daughters to find a little universe hidden in a tide pool. I carry countless memories of this world in my heart—the Eiffel Tower lit up at night, a field of wild flowers in the Swiss Alps with a chorus of wooden cowbells chiming in the distance, and a ruined abbey with red sandstone walls, the sky for a ceiling, and a floor of perfectly mowed grass. I've seen a bloodred moon rise over the desert, and I've slid down natural waterslides in jungle rivers. I delight in all the cultures that share this world, each with its own language, food, customs, and art. A thousand years wouldn't be enough time to experience all of them.

I love the wonder and beauty of this world, natural and man-made. So it crushes me to think of it being burned up, never to be enjoyed again. Everything here is going to be destroyed and the human soul is the only thing that really matters. That's what we believe, right?

Does that bother you? It bothers me. I love creation and hate the thought of seeing it destroyed. I also hate the apathy this doctrine encourages. Many Christians are suspicious of environmentalism. We are frequently hostile to art. Many evangelicals believe that physical training is of no value.[2] Christians were once at the forefront of caring for those in need, but fear of being associated with liberal causes keeps many conservatives on the sidelines. No wonder our belief in heaven is so unappealing to the world. So what's the radically normal perspective on how this world ends?

Renewal or Destruction?

Of course, whether I like a particular doctrine is absolutely irrelevant. Just because I can't understand or appreciate something is no gauge of its veracity. But is the common view of heaven accurate? Christians have disagreed about the end times for a long, long time. Views that are popular now used to be considered fringe and vice versa. I lack the knowledge and the inclination to wade into that debate. All

I want to do is reevaluate the popular "it's all going to burn and I'm going to fly away" apocalyptic theology.

Does the Bible teach that God is going to crumple up and throw away this physical world and save only the souls? The short answer is no.

> Creation isn't waiting eagerly to be destroyed, but to be renewed.

The Old Testament prophets proclaimed that God would renew and restore this world instead.[3] Jesus confirmed this when he spoke of the renewal of all things, not their destruction.

> Jesus said to them, "Truly I tell you, at the renewal of all things, when the Son of Man sits on his glorious throne, you who have followed me will also sit on twelve thrones, judging the twelve tribes of Israel" (Matthew 19:28).[4]

But what about apocalyptic passages that indicate that everything is going to be destroyed, such as 2 Peter 3:10? "But the day of the Lord will come like a thief. The heavens will disappear with a roar; the elements will be destroyed by fire, and the earth and everything done in it will be laid bare."

> Do you think God looks at his creation as a rough draft or the first chapter of his great adventure?

First, notice something strange. If the elements have been destroyed, how is the earth still around to be "laid bare" (literally "discovered")? Apparently it hasn't been completely destroyed after all.[5] Peter is simply using apocalyptic language to describe the inescapability of God's judgment.[6] So what happens to the earth? This is what Paul tells us.

> For the creation waits in eager expectation for the children of God to be revealed. For the creation was subjected to frustration, not by its own choice, but by the will of the one who subjected it, in hope that the creation itself will be liberated from its bondage to decay and brought into the freedom and glory of the children of God (Romans 8:19-21).

Clearly, creation isn't waiting eagerly to be destroyed, but to be renewed, liberated from decay. Maybe this passage helps answer one of the most vexing theological questions of our age—do our pets go to heaven? We still can't answer that with confidence, though I once had a Siamese cat that I'm pretty sure went to hell. However, this does teach that creation itself goes to heaven. I say that tongue in cheek because the Bible seems to say that creation actually *becomes* heaven.

> Then I saw "a new heaven and a new earth," for the first heaven and the first earth had passed away, and there was no longer any sea. I saw the Holy City, the new Jerusalem, coming down out of heaven from God, prepared as a bride beautifully dressed for her husband. And I heard a loud voice from the throne saying, "Look! God's dwelling place is now among the people, and he will dwell with them. They will be his people, and God himself will be with them and be their God. 'He will wipe every tear from their eyes. There will be no more death' or mourning or crying or pain, for the old order of things has passed away" (Revelation 21:1-4).

Putting everything the Bible says together, the picture seems to be that God will renew heaven (which basically means "the skies" in this context) and earth and then move the new Jerusalem to the renewed earth. That is why I said at the end of chapter 16 that we won't spend eternity in heaven—we'll spend it with God on the new earth.[7] This is no mere technicality. What we believe about the future profoundly affects the way we live now.

The First Chapter

One of the most important writing skills I've acquired is allowing myself to write really crummy rough drafts (author Anne Lamott has a more colorful phrase for it). The early drafts of this book were absolute garbage, but I had to start somewhere. Through practice and countless revisions, I ended up with something I'm excited to share. A disproportionate amount of time went into the first chapter—I probably revised it more than 25 times. That is because the first chapter is the most important one of any book. It introduces the theme and makes the reader curious enough to keep reading. How many books have you put back on the shelf after losing interest on page 3?

Let me ask you this. Do you think God looks at his creation as a rough draft or as the first chapter of his great adventure, "which goes on forever: in which every chapter is better than the one before"?[8] Somehow, I don't think God needed a rough draft—he told us himself that he thought it was pretty good. Some people think the Fall damaged creation beyond repair, but I think that seriously underestimates God's redemptive power.

Let me ask you another question. Do you treat this life as a rough draft that will be thrown away or as the first chapter of your own great adventure? Do you believe, as I do, that what we do here will have profound implications on the rest of our story? I'm not talking about whether you prayed the sinner's prayer.

> For no one can lay any foundation other than the one already laid, which is Jesus Christ. If anyone builds on this foundation using gold, silver, costly stones, wood, hay or straw, their work will be shown for what it is, because the Day will bring it to light. It will be revealed with fire, and the fire will test the quality of each person's work. If what has been built survives, the builder will receive a reward. If it is burned up, the builder will suffer loss but yet will be saved—even though only as one escaping through the flames (1 Corinthians 3:11-15).

This verse isn't talking about whether or not you are saved; Paul is speaking to those who are building on "the foundation of Christ." Likewise, he says that Christians will have to appear before the judgment seat of Christ to "receive what is due [us] for the things done while in the body, whether good or bad" (2 Corinthians 5:10). If you've been living like heaven is a big do-over, that can be a very unsettling verse!

Complacent, nearsighted Christianity treats this life and this world as all there is without giving serious consideration to the next. Complacent Christians will arrive in heaven and find themselves completely unprepared. On the other hand, obsessive, farsighted Christians treat this life as a necessary evil to be endured while waiting for heaven. Being radically normal means fully enjoying and engaging in this life, knowing it has profound and multifaceted implications on eternity.

Matter That Matters

Look at it this way. Is our salvation a current reality or a future hope? Actually, it's both. Even while you look forward to your complete renewal and purification, you can already be experiencing God's transforming work in your life. In the same way, God's renewal of creation is both a future promise and present reality. Creation is waiting for its liberation from decay, but God has already begun renewing this world, and (this is the important part) he's doing it through us. We know that God spreads the gospel through us, but Scripture also says that he cares for the poor, heals the hurting, and tends the creation through us.[9]

When we combine these two truths—that our earthly actions have eternal consequences and that God is going to renew this world through us—we come away with a very important realization. What we do here matters. What we do with our bodies matters, caring for others matters, art matters, and this earth matters.

Our Bodies Matter

Our culture normally bases our value on our bodies. Does that mean Christians shouldn't care about their bodies at all? Apparently that's what a lot of us think. One study showed that young adults who attend church regularly are 50 percent more likely to be obese than their unchurched counterparts.[10] Why is that? My theory is that gluttony is our most acceptable vice. A pastor can make a joke about being gluttonous at the potluck and everyone will laugh, but if he makes a joke about lusting over Sister Bertha in her low-cut dress, he'll be looking for a new job. Christians routinely seem to undervalue their earthly bodies. God, however, does not.

> Do you not know that your bodies are temples of the Holy
> Spirit, who is in you, whom you have received from God?

> You are not your own; you were bought at a price. There-
> fore honor God with your bodies (1 Corinthians 6:19-20).

Contrary to how I learned it, this isn't the Bible's antismoking verse.
The point is far bigger than that. Our bodies are where the Holy Spirit
dwells. They are his temples and should be treated as such.

One of the most important doctrines of the early church was the
resurrection and transformation of our actual bodies. It's not simply
our souls that live forever but our (renewed) bodies as well.

> So will it be with the resurrection of the dead. The body
> that is sown is perishable, it is raised imperishable; it is
> sown in dishonor, it is raised in glory; it is sown in weak-
> ness, it is raised in power; it is sown a natural body, it is
> raised a spiritual body (1 Corinthians 15:42-44).

Just as Jesus was raised with a real body that could be seen, could be
touched, and could (oh glory!) eat, so shall we be (Luke 24:36-43). His
resurrection body was more real than his previous body, not less.

But what about the story where Jesus seems to pass through a
locked door (John 20:26)? Here's my theory.
Jesus could walk through that door because he **The way you**
was more solid than it was. Think about it this **treat your**
way—you and I can wade through water with **body speaks**
ease. Is that because we're less solid than water? **very loudly.**
Just the opposite. We're so much more "real" than
water, it has to move for us and then close up behind us. That's kind of
freaky when you think about it—maybe you and I are the ones who
are ghostlike compared to the reality of heaven![11]

Why is the bodily resurrection so important? Many reasons, including the possibility that how you treat your natural body will have some
sort of implications for your resurrection body. After all, Jesus kept his
scars—they are now badges of honor. Perhaps the disabilities of people like Joni Erickson Tada, who bears being a quadriplegic with grace,
will be transformed into crowns of glory. On the other hand, perhaps
those who abuse and misuse their bodies will "suffer loss." If you can't

be faithful with God's most basic gift of your body, what *can* he trust you with?

The way you treat your body speaks very loudly. It might say that you lack discipline and self-control. It might say, through immodesty, that you care more about attracting attention than honoring God. It might say, through obsessive exercise, that your body is your idol. Or it might say that food and pleasure are. I want the way I treat my body to say that I gratefully enjoyed it and honored it as God's dwelling place.

Caring for Others Matters

Let's say you had to give away $1000. You could either give it to a Christian organization that you knew hypothetically would save five souls, or you could give it to a secular organization that you knew would save fifty girls from the sex trade. Which one should you choose? According to the theology I grew up with, the Christian organization should get the money. What's the point of saving the girls if they will go to hell?

That seems to make a weird kind of sense, but it's out of harmony with what the Bible actually says. Nowhere does Scripture say caring for someone's earthly needs is pointless if we don't save their souls. The Bible has a deep interest in caring for people—speaking for those who cannot speak for themselves, freeing the oppressed, feeding the hungry, and comforting the suffering—even apart from evangelism. Having learned more about God's heart for "the least of these," I gratefully accepted the opportunity to serve the homeless at the Friendship House and am honored to continue to do so.

Don't get me wrong. I believe the gospel reveals the only path to complete healing and restoration. The point is that God expects us to relieve both physical and spiritual poverty. Loren Cunningham, founder of Youth with a Mission, talked about the two hands of the gospel, meaning that we must care for both body and soul. I believe that this is a biblical model worth pursuing.

Art and Beauty Matter

The church was once the champion of art and beauty, from Handel's *Messiah* to Saint Peter's Basilica. Now many Christians see such things as a waste of time and money. Every time megachurches build expensive buildings, loud voices condemn them, asking how they can spend that much money on temporary buildings instead of missions and the poor. That seems like a biblical objection, right?

Consider this. The tabernacle had 3.75 tons of silver and more than a ton of gold, easily making it the world's most expensive tent (Exodus 38:24-25). Solomon's temple was even more impressive, yet nowhere does the Bible complain that the money should have been given to the poor or spent on missions. Rather, it brags about the extravagance and expenses. Israel believed that the one true God should have a truly glorious dwelling place because it was meant to mirror his glory in some small way.

Likewise, when Marilyn and I went to Jerusalem, we saw many ancient churches that were gaudy to our tastes. But the Orthodox Christians who worship there believe that their buildings should give them a glimpse of the beauty of heaven. They would probably find most evangelical churches austere and sterile.

Wasn't that just in the Old Testament? The early church didn't even have their own church buildings, right? That's true, but did they believe they shouldn't construct buildings, or did Christianity's questionable legal status prevent them from doing so? I don't know, but I do know that the Bible never condemns church buildings, so perhaps we should be cautious in our judgments.

Of course, I'm not justifying every opulent church. I can't comment on a particular church's building budget because it's none of my business. My only point is that spending money (even a lot of money) on beauty isn't necessarily wrong.

Now, regarding art—when we combine the biblical examples of displaying God's glory with the prophetic role of proclaiming truth, I believe we have a very strong case for the church returning to its role as a major supporter of the arts in all of its mediums. That is not to say that Christian art always has to be nice and pretty. Just as the Old Testament prophets sometimes had to be pretty disturbing to tell the truth, so also Christian artists may also be called to shock us.

This Earth Matters

As I said, Christians have frequently been behind the rest of the world when it comes to caring for the environment. Many fear being associated with a certain political party or the New Age movement. Our popular apocalyptic theology doesn't help. Fortunately this is changing, but I lament that we're following the world's example rather leading the way. God loves his creation (just read Job 38–41), and we should feel humbled and privileged that he entrusted it to our care. Rather than treat this world like a hotel room that someone else will clean up, we should treat it like a lakeside cabin that our boss let us borrow for the weekend. How we treat it shows God how much he can trust us with his other things.

Not in Vain

I wish I could have spent more time on each of those topics—each deserves its own book. Fortunately, many good books have been written (see the suggested reading list for a few of them). But to wrap this all up, I want to quote from *Surprised by Hope*, which inspired this chapter. N.T. Wright passionately conveyed what it means to be agents of God's renewal of this earth.

> What you do in the Lord is *not in vain*. You are not oiling the wheels of a machine that's about to roll over a cliff. You are not restoring a great painting that's shortly going to be thrown on the fire. You are not planting roses in a garden that's about to be dug up for a building site. You are— strange though it may seem, almost as hard to believe as the resurrection itself—accomplishing something that will become in due course part of God's new world. Every act of love, gratitude, and kindness; every work of art or music inspired by the love of God and delight in the beauty of his creation; every minute spent teaching a severely handicapped child to read or to walk; every act of care and nurture, of comfort and support, for one's fellow human beings and for that matter one's fellow nonhuman creatures; and

of course every prayer, all Spirit-led teaching, every deed that spreads the gospel, builds up the church, embraces and embodies holiness rather than corruption, and makes the name of Jesus honored in the world—all of this will find its way, through the resurrecting power of God, into the new creation that God will one day make.[12]

I have a friend who was invited to speak at Def Con, a conference for computer hackers and those who try to stop them. He was reluctant to accept the invitation because he knew his presentation could help the "bad guys." In the end, he realized that by addressing some major holes in the system, he'd do more good than harm.

In the final chapter, you'll see why I can relate to my friend. Some may use this book to justify their complacent Christianity, but I believe it has an even greater potential to help you follow Jesus more closely.

Onward

In the fall of 2012, I began to sense that my time at Starbucks would be ending soon, and I was a little frightened by the thought. I spent a night wrestling with God and realized that once I was back in full-time ministry, I'd lose my excuses. For 18 months, whenever someone asked why this or that was wrong with the church, I blamed working at Starbucks. For good reason—I was stretched very thin in those days. But I was afraid of the increased expectations that might accompany returning to full-time ministry. I was afraid that I couldn't measure up. "The Starbucks era" had undoubtedly been one of the most important seasons in my life, yet I had to face the fact that I was allowing it to hold me back. Eventually, I surrendered my excuses and self-doubt to God. "If you took me this far, Father, I can trust you to take me through the next stage too."

Less than three weeks later, I stood in front of my congregation and told them that it was my last Sunday as a bivocational pastor. An unexpected change in our church's finances (a story in itself) allowed me to quit Starbucks and return to being a full-time pastor. I was no longer afraid, but eager and excited for what was ahead. That Sunday, I preached a sermon titled "Lessons I Learned at Starbucks." I decided to preach it wearing my green Starbucks apron, partially for the drama of taking it off at the end, but more as a final assault on any embarrassment I still had over my "normal" job.

The final lesson of that sermon was deeply personal. I told my church that I hadn't realized how fortunate I was to be their pastor. I didn't appreciate what I had until it was nearly taken away. I got choked up as I talked about that year and a half at Starbucks. By God's grace, we had stuck together through many trials, and now it was time to move forward. I took my apron off and asked, "So where do we go from here?"

> The Master was far more pleased by what they did with what they were given than he was with the net profit.

I write this final chapter in that same spirit. Thank you for sticking with me through these chapters and allowing me to talk with you. I hope these lessons and stories have impacted you as they've impacted me, but now it's time to move forward. This book isn't the final word, but only a jumping-off point. I trust the Holy Spirit to take you onward. I'll leave you with seven specific challenges to help you avoid both obsessive and complacent Christianity and discover the radically normal life God wants to give to you.

1. Examine Your Pursuit of God

Remember that there are not two separate tiers of Christianity, with the super-Christians on top and the rest of us on the bottom. There is only the "saved by grace and not by works" tier, and it includes John the Baptist, the apostle Paul, Mother Teresa, Billy Graham, you, and me. We are all in it together.

> On a scale of one to five (one meaning not at all and five meaning completely), how honestly can you say, "By his grace, I'm pursuing wholehearted devotion to God"?
>
> 1   2   3   4   5

If you answered anything less than a five, ask yourself why. If your answer is "Because I don't want to," at least you're being honest. An answer like "Because I can't" is nothing less than a lie of the enemy.

Every believer's walk is empowered by God's grace, which each of us is capable of receiving. The only thing required on your end to circle a five is surrender.

2. Discover Your Greatness

I want you to be welcomed into heaven with the words "Well done, good and faithful servant!" Do you know the context of those words of praise? It's from the parable of the talents (Matthew 25:14-30). As you may remember, one servant started with five talents and earned five more, and another started with two talents and earned two more. Have you ever noticed that both of them receive exactly the same praise, word for word? The Master was far more pleased by what they did with what they were given than he was with the net profit. I find that very encouraging because it means God's definition of greatness is different from my own. The only servant who was rebuked was the one who didn't do anything with his talent.

Your opportunity for greatness comes from finding the talents God has given to you and then partnering with him. Don't worry about everyone else; just pursue the greatness God has given you. Remember, "The place God calls you to is where your deep gladness and the world's deep hunger meet."[1]

If you don't already know what your deep gladness is, commit yourself to discovering it and finding out how you can meet the world's hunger through it. (See appendix 2 for some resources.)

That's only the first step. Greatness does not come easy. Ask yourself what you may need to sacrifice to pursue your calling. I had to make a daily choice to write instead of getting a high score on my favorite video game. The choice sounds so obvious now, but in the moment I had all sorts of excuses—I needed to wind down, I deserved a break, I'd only play for five minutes, and so on. In the end, I had to delete that game from my computer. Had I not made that sacrifice, I wouldn't have written this book.

Is *sacrifice* really the right word? I gave up a mindless video game to pursue my lifelong dream. The lesser joy is not worth comparing to the greater joy. I still play an occasional video game and watch an

NORMAL

occasional TV show, but pursing my greatness cost me some of my leisure time.

Where do your deep gladness and the world's hunger meet?

_____

What might you need to sacrifice in order to pursue your greatness?

_____

3. Enjoy This Life

Spiritual joys are not better than earthly joys—there is a proper time and place to enjoy each. If you think God is happier when you're praying than when you're watching a football game, you'll be far less likely to invite him to the game. And when you don't invite Jesus to the football game, bad things are more likely to happen there.

Take a moment to think about what you enjoy doing. On a scale of one to five, how frequently do you invite Jesus to join you there?

1   2   3   4   5

If you didn't mark five, consider why. Do you struggle to believe that God really wants you to enjoy this life? Or do you know, deep down, that your fun isn't entirely sin free? As I said before, my goal is for you to be able to scream your lungs out over a touchdown one moment and whisper a "Thank you, Jesus" the next.

4. Pursue Happy Holiness

Sin is fun—at first. But in the end, it will leave you miserable. Holiness isn't always easy, but it brings greater joy. Do you believe that God has your best interests in mind? Pursue holiness by creating your own Consequence Inverter. Commit to trusting God's wisdom more than your own.

Identify one sin you're holding onto. Are you ready to start trusting

God and believing that obedience brings joy? If so, begin with the simple prayer, "I do believe; help me overcome my unbelief!"

But happy holiness isn't just about what you stop doing, it's also about what you start doing.

> What is one new spiritual discipline you want to begin exercising?
>
> silence and solitude
>
> prayer
>
> fasting
>
> Bible reading
>
> church participation

5. Grow in Generosity

Generosity is a great way to experience joy through obedience, but it's the hardest one for many of us. Neither complacent accumulation nor obsessive sacrifice is the biblical ideal. We are blessed to be a blessing—God is generous to us so that we can enjoy some and give some. In doing so, he also tests our ability to handle more important things.

> On a scale of one to five, how much do you think God can bless you and know that others will be blessed thorough you?
>
> 1   2   3   4   5

If you can't mark five, consider why not. Remember that a five doesn't mean you have to give everything away. It usually means being like the Proverbs 31 woman, who opened her arms to the poor yet enjoyed the fruits of her labor. Are you willing to ask God to help you find joy in generosity? If so, begin by identifying one new opportunity to practice generosity. You may have to sacrifice some lesser joys in order to gain greater ones.

6. Cultivate Hunger

The joys of this life can either distract you from Jesus or help you long for him more. God has put a heaven-shaped hole in you to keep you from getting too comfortable here. If you try to numb these eternal hunger pains with earthly things, the earthly joys will distract and disappoint you. Instead, cultivate this hunger. Then they can become samples of eternal joy and help you long for God.

> On a scale of one to five, how much do you enjoy this life but long for the next?

1   2   3   4   5

If you didn't answer five, do you struggle more with enjoying this life or longing for the next? Do you need to cultivate hunger by fasting, or do you need to cultivate joy by embracing the good things of this life?

7. Live Like It Matters

This life is not a rough draft. God is not going to destroy it and start over. It's the first chapter of his great story. How we live this life has profound implications for the next. What we do here matters.

> On a scale of one to five, how much do you welcome the news that this life is only the first chapter?

1   2   3   4   5

If you didn't answer five, consider why. Are you nervous that your poor stewardship of your body, your resources, and this planet will cause you to suffer loss in eternity?

I challenge you to choose just one area of this life to pay more attention to—your body, caring for the poor and oppressed, promoting art and beauty, or caring for the environment.

We Can Do This

You might have assumed I wrote this book in reaction to other books that promote a more obsessive form of Christianity. That is not the case. I probably share a common goal with those authors. I think we have all witnessed the tragedy of complacent Christianity and are desperate to rescue God's people from it. The biggest difference between this book and some others is in our strategies. Perhaps some authors set such high standards in order to move us just a little closer. Maybe they would be happy if they could simply get average Christians to start tithing and talking to their neighbors about Jesus.

> I'm making wholehearted devotion harder by making it possible.

There are two problems with obsessive goals. First, they are misleading. As you now know, I don't think obsessive Christianity is biblical. Second, they don't work. In my experience, most Christians read that kind of book and feel guilty for not measuring up, but they don't change. Instead, I've tried to motivate by showing that wholehearted obedience brings greater joy.

I've also tried to remove the biggest excuse and fear that most of us have—"I can't do this." Perhaps I'll be accused of tickling itching ears, encouraging complacency, removing the sacrifice, and making Christianity too easy. Don't believe that for a minute. I'm actually making wholehearted devotion harder by making it possible. Did you notice that I expected you to mark a five on all of the "one to five" questions? God's grace makes every one of us capable of being a fully committed follower of Christ. Nothing you've read requires a move to India or vow of poverty. If I've done my job, you haven't been thinking, "It's nice that pastors and missionaries can follow Jesus like that." Instead, I hope you've been thinking, "I can do this." Being radically normal isn't easy, but it's certainly achievable through (and only through) God's grace. What's more, it's a lot more joy filled than being obsessive or complacent.

Happy Endings

I ended the first chapter with the story of telling Grace and Sarah that we were taking them to Disneyland. Two months after my final Starbucks sermon, the four of us were on a plane headed for Southern

California. I had been praying about the trip and preparing for it for years, and God's generosity blew us away. No one who earns as little as I did should be able to give his family the sort of vacation we had. Blessing after blessing was poured out on us, even before we got to Disneyland.

Perhaps my favorite memory is of the ride from the airport to the hotel. For the same price as a taxi, I was able to surprise my little princesses (and their mommy) with their first limo ride. They giggled with delight as they drank 7-Up from champagne glasses and watched the interior lights change colors. I held back tears of joy and gratitude. The driver took us to In-N-Out Burger, and we ate a late dinner in the limo as she gave us an extended ride through Anaheim. I tipped her very well.

The next day was amazing. The lines were short, and we got to go on almost every ride. Marilyn's ticket had a picture of Bambi, her favorite Disney character. It was as if God winked at her. Thanks to a gift from a dear friend, we were able to do all the things I never got to do as a kid, including buying autograph books and eating wherever we wanted. We also got great pictures of the girls with Tinker Bell in Pixie Hollow. That night, as I tucked Grace and Sarah into bed and kissed them goodnight, I didn't bother asking them their favorite part of the day. I already knew the answer—all of it. As they fell asleep, I took a moment just to look at them, so precious in my sight. I was so happy that I could bring them so much joy.

God is always good, but his goodness is more tangible at some times than at others. I didn't regret the trials he had taken us through, but I was grateful for the moments of delight. As I fell asleep, I knew that my Father was also watching me, so precious in his sight, happy that he could bring me so much joy.

Join the Conversation

I'd love for you to follow me on Twitter (@joshkelley) and visit my website and blog at www.RadicallyNormal.com. If you'd like to join the conversation about being radically normal, use the hashtag #RadicallyNormal or respond to some of my blog posts. Better yet, start your own conversation!

Questions for Group Discussion or Personal Reflection

To get the most out of your group discussion or personal reflection on each chapter, begin your time with prayer, asking God to guide you. Then answer this general question: What was the one thing you want to remember the most from this chapter?

After using these questions below, end your time by answering this question: What's the one thing you want to do differently based on what you've learned? Then close with prayer, asking for God's help.

Chapter 1: Obsessive and Complacent Christianity

1. Describe obsessive and complacent Christianity in your own words.

2. Do you struggle more with being obsessive or complacent?

3. Why did Josh say that he'd prefer that you were complacent rather than obsessive? Do you agree or disagree?

4. Have you ever hoped that Christianity wasn't true? Why?

5. Do you struggle to view God as a loving Father (*Abba*)? How might your view of God affect your ability to enjoy this life?

6. What do you hope to gain from this study?

Chapter 2: Grasping Grace

1. Did this chapter change your understanding of grace? If so, how?

2. Josh said that your biggest responsibility in your Christian walk is to let Jesus carry you. Do you agree or disagree? How can this idea be taken too far?

3. Describe the two cliffs in your own words.

4. Which cliff presents the biggest danger to you? Has it always been that way?

Chapter 3: It's Okay to Be Normal

1. Have you known a Radical Randy? If so, how has this person affected your desire to follow God?

2. What does reading the Bible contextually mean? Why is it important?

3. Do you think being radical is overemphasized in the church today? In what ways is being radical good? In what ways is it bad?

4. Have you ever found your identity in being a better Christian than other people? How does that affect your relationship with God? With other Christians?

5. Have you ever felt like a minor-league Christian? Have you ever used that to excuse halfhearted obedience?

Chapter 4: Honorable Work

1. Describe a time you struggled to find significance in your job.

2. Have you ever used not being in vocational ministry as an excuse for not serving God?

3. If you are or have been in vocational ministry, have you been guilty of elevating your calling above others?

4. In your own words, explain the relationship Josh sees between the Old and New Testaments. Do you agree or disagree? Why?

5. Does this view of the Old Testament make you more interested in reading it? If so, what are some steps you could take to do so?

6. What are the two Great Commissions Josh described? Does the first Great Commission affect how you feel about work? If so, how?

Chapter 5: Greatness for Average Joes

1. Whom have you compared yourself to as a Christian?

2. What are the two types of low ambitions Josh talked about? Which one is a greater temptation for you?

3. What are you good at? If you can't answer that, what do other people say you're good at? How can you discover your strengths and build on them?

4. If you could do anything for God and knew you couldn't fail, what would you do?

5. What books and stories inspire you to greatness?

Chapter 6: Why Are Christians So Weird?

1. Did you grow up in a Christian subculture? If so, do you remember it with fondness, embarrassment, or bitterness?

2. Has fear of appearing odd ever held you back from following God?

3. What are the benefits of not being a part of the popular culture? What are the disadvantages?

4. Many people believe that America is becoming a post-Christian nation. In what ways is that a bad thing? In what ways is it good?

5. Do you believe Halloween can be redeemed for good? Why or why not? If yes, what are some ways to do so?

6. In what ways should and shouldn't we look strange to non-Christians?

Chapter 7: Witnessing Without Weirdness

1. Share about an experience you had witnessing. Was it a positive or negative experience?

2. Read Titus 2:10. What does Paul mean when he says, "They will make the teachings about God our Savior attractive"? How can you do that?

3. Do you struggle more with speaking about God when you should be quiet or keeping quiet when you should speak?

4. Read 1 Peter 3:15-16. What elements of evangelism are imbedded in this passage?

Chapter 8: In Defense of Earthly Joys

1. Do you think the average non-Christian thinks of Christians as joy filled or joyless? Why?

2. Have you divided your life into earthly and spiritual compartments? If so, describe them.

3. What are some biblical passages that praise earthly joy?

4. What are some ways you can balance seeking God with enjoying his gifts?

5. Josh challenged you to invite Jesus to the football game. What does that mean for you? How can you do that?

Chapter 9: When God Throws a Party

1. Are your celebrations more inclined to be complacently sinful or obsessively religious?

2. What are some ways that sin makes parties less fun?

3. What did Josh mean when he suggested you infuse joy and meaning into events? What are some practical ways you can do that?

4. Describe a celebration that would help you look forward to heaven.

Chapter 10: In Defense of Spiritual Joys

1. Does enjoying God and his presence come naturally for you, or is it a struggle?

2. How can earthly enjoyment help you enjoy God more?

3. What are the five spiritual disciplines that Josh discussed? What would you add to that list? Which ones are easiest for you? Which are hardest?

4. Read through the list of sacred pathways. Which ones resonate with you the most?

5. How did Josh describe balancing earthly and spiritual joys? Which one do you need to emphasize more right now?

Chapter 11: Happy Holiness

1. Josh described sin as short-lived pleasure at the expense of long-term happiness. How would you illustrate that using a personal experience?

2. What was Satan's lie about God? What are some ways you've bought into that lie?

3. Josh said that obeying God is the best path to joy. Can you think of any apparent exceptions to that?

4. What was the Consequence Inverter? How can you create one of your own?

5. Why did Josh say that all sins are, at their core, sins of unbelief? Do you agree or disagree?

Chapter 12: What About Money?

1. Describe a time when you felt guilty for spending money on yourself.

2. What is consumerism? What are some of the ways you've bought into it?

3. What are some of the good things the Bible says about money? What are some of the warnings it gives?

4. What are the three safe practices Josh gave for handling money? Which one is most important for you to start using?

5. Why did Josh say that generosity is not optional for Christians? Do you agree or disagree?

6. How did Josh say you can know whether you're being generous enough?

Chapter 13: Between Legalism and Worldliness, Part 1

1. What did Josh mean by the word *fences*? What are some fences in your life?

2. Why did Josh say fences provide only an illusion of safety? Do you agree or disagree?

3. What are some ways you've tried to put fences along other peoples' paths?

4. Describe a time you felt patronized because of your fences or judged for your lack of them.

Chapter 14: Between Legalism and Worldliness, Part 2

1. What are some of the biblical meanings of the phrase *the world*? Describe a time that you hated the wrong world.

2. How would you describe worldliness?

3. Read 1 Thessalonians 5:19-22. How can you apply this verse to avoiding worldliness?

4. How can you decide which movies, shows, books, or games are so harmful that you must avoid them entirely? How does this standard change for different people?

5. How much time do you spend on entertainment? Is that amount of time appropriate?

Chapter 15: Don't Waste Pain

1. What does Ecclesiastes mean by "Sorrow is better than laughter" (7:3)?

2. What are some lessons you've learned in pain?

3. What did Josh mean by using suffering to find joy?

4. Read Romans 8:28-30. What does it teach you about your suffering?

5. Do you find God's answer to Job comforting? Why or why not?

6. What did Josh mean by saying we tend to numb our pain? What are some destructive ways you've tried to numb your pain?

Chapter 16: Hungry for Heaven

1. Have earthly joys distracted you from eternity or made you long for Jesus more?

2. What are eternal hunger pains? Describe a time when you felt them.

3. What did Josh mean when he said it's okay to be hungry?

4. How have you tried to numb your eternal hunger pains?

5. What are some ways you can cultivate hunger? What are some ways you can cultivate joy?

Chapter 17: This Life Matters

1. Do you view this life more like a rough draft or a first chapter? How do you think that affects how you live?

2. What are the eternal consequences of how you treat your earthly body?

3. Would you give the $1000 to the Christian organization that saved five souls or the secular organization that saved fifty girls from the sex trade? Why?

4. Do you think it's okay for churches to spend a lot of money on their buildings? Why or why not?

5. What are some God-honoring ways you can better care for this earth?

Chapter 18: Onward

1. Begin by using the six questions in chapter 18.

2. How has this book changed you?

3. What do you wish the book would have covered that it did not?

4. What are the top three ways you want to be more radically normal a year from now? (Consider using www.FutureMe .org to send yourself an email one year from now.)

Appendix 2

Suggested Reading List

As I said in chapter 18, this book is a jumping-off point. Here is a list of books you might find useful. It's an eclectic list of books that have shaped my thinking or have been recommended by people I trust. Of course, you shouldn't assume that I agree with everything in every book listed here.

Chapter 1: Obsessive and Complacent Christianity

"The Weight of Glory," chapter 1 in *The Weight of Glory: And Other Addresses* by C.S. Lewis. One of my all-time favorite sermons.

Accidental Pharisees: Avoiding Pride, Exclusivity, and the Other Dangers of Overzealous Faith by Larry Osborne. This is a good book if you want to read more about the cliff of legalism.

Chapter 2: Grasping Grace

Galatians for You by Timothy Keller and *Galatians for Everyone* by N.T. Wright. These are good, brief commentaries for the average reader. My sermon series on Galatians can be found by clicking on "Resources" at www.RadicallyNormal.com.

Classic Christianity by Bob George.

Chapter 3: It's Okay to Be Normal

The God of the Mundane by Matthew B. Redmond. I love the title of this book. It was written by another pastor who found himself back in the workplace.

How to Read the Bible for All Its Worth by Gordon Fee and Douglas Stuart. This is the best introduction to studying, interpreting, and applying the Bible that I've found.

Studying, Interpreting, and Applying the Bible by Walter Henrichsen and Gayle Jackson. A little bit dated but still very useful.

The Blue Parakeet: Rethinking How You Read the Bible by Scot McKnight. A great book on how to stop ignoring difficult Bible passages and start learning from them.

Chapter 4: Honorable Work

"On Learning in Wartime," chapter 2 in *The Weight of Glory: And Other Addresses* by C.S. Lewis. In this address, Lewis answers the question, how can we do anything other than win souls?

Every Good Endeavor by Timothy Keller.

Up from Slavery by Booker T. Washington. A fascinating autobiography and ode to the value of hard work.

Here are some good resources for better enjoying and understanding the Old Testament:

The Bible Jesus Read by Philip Yancey.

A Reflection on the Psalms by C.S. Lewis.

Delighting in the Law of the Lord by Jerram Barrs.

Chapter 5: Greatness for Average Joes

A Million Miles in a Thousand Years by Donald Miller. This will inspire you to sacrifice lesser things for greater joy.

Do Hard Things by Alex and Brett Harris. This book calls teens and preteens to stop hiding behind their age and do great things for God.

Quitters by Jonathan Acuff. If you want to quit your day job to pursue your calling, read this book first. Acuff's advice will help you do so wisely.

Strength Finders 2.0 by Tom Rath. This book includes access to the best assessment tool for discovering your strengths I've ever found. My wife will tell you that it changed her life. Be sure to get a new copy with an unused access code.

When a Woman Discovers Her Dream by Cindi McMenamin.

Chapter 6: Why Are Christians So Weird?

Real Christians Don't Dance: Sorting the Truth from the Trappings in a Born-Again Culture by John Fischer. This book might be a little dated, but it set me free from the Christian subculture.

Stuff Christians Like by Jonathan Acuff. Pokes fun at us without being caustic.

Chapter 7: Witnessing Without Weirdness

Going Public with Your Faith: Becoming a Spiritual Influence at Work by Bill Peel and Walt Larimore.

Neighbors and Wise Men by Tony Kriz. Can God speak to you through the very people with whom you want to share Jesus? I believe he can, and we would be foolish to be so busy talking that we can't listen. My friend Tony's book is a well-told story of how God spoke to him through unexpected people.

Chapter 8: In Defense of Earthly Joys

Pure Pleasure: Why Do Christians Feel So Bad about Feeling Good? by Gary Thomas. My chapter was the tip of the iceberg on proper enjoyment of earthly things. Thomas's book dives much deeper.

God and the Art of Happiness by Ellen T. Charry. This book is a little on the technical side, but it was foundational in helping me understand the biblical role of earthly joy, why happiness is the proper motivation for obedience, and how the church came to mistakenly value disinterested obedience.

Desiring God: Meditations of a Christian Hedonist by John Piper. The basic thesis is that we glorify God by enjoying him. I love Piper's emphasis on pursuing God out of delight, but I wish he'd say more about the proper role of earthly joys.

Lost Virtue of Happiness by J.P. Moreland and Klaus Issler. This book does a good job of clarifying the difference between happiness and instant gratification.

Chapter 9: When God Throws a Party

"Xmas and Christmas: A Lost Chapter from Herodotus," part 3, chapter 5 in *God in the Dock* by C.S. Lewis. A great satirical piece on Christmas and consumerism.

Chapter 10: In Defense of Spiritual Joys

The Purpose Driven Life by Rick Warren. For a basic entry-level guide to the Christian life, this book is hard to beat. Christians who dismiss its principles as too elementary might benefit from its practices.

A Resilient Life and *Ordering Your Private World* by Gordon MacDonald. I highly recommend both of these books for helping you find health and balance in your life.

Life Together by Dietrich Bonhoeffer. A great look at biblical community. It has an excellent chapter on the confession of sins.

Called to Stay by Caleb Breakey. My friend Caleb challenges Christians to stop complaining about the church and start loving it.

Celebration of Discipline by Richard J. Foster. This is the classic book about spiritual disciplines.

Practice of the Presence of God by Brother Lawrence. I love the way this short, classic book encourages us to seek God's presence even in the most mundane things. On the other hand, it can inadvertently downplay the value of the mundane things in themselves.

Letters to Malcolm: Chiefly on Prayer by C.S. Lewis. If not understanding how prayer works hinders you, this book may help you as it helped me.

Sacred Pathways by Gary Thomas. This is the book that helped me discover how I'm wired to experience God's presence, and I think you'll find it very helpful as well.

Chapter 11: Happy Holiness

Love Your God with All Your Mind: The Role of Reason in the Life of the Soul by J.P. Moreland. The value of wisdom and clear thinking in the life of a believer is hard to overestimate. Moreland attempts to restore their importance among evangelical Christians.

The Screwtape Letters by C.S. Lewis. A great book about the nature of sin and temptation.

The Great Divorce by C.S. Lewis. A brilliant book about sin and righteousness disguised as an entertaining story about a trip to heaven and hell.

Hole in Our Holiness by Kevin DeYoung. A great book about holiness and why it matters.

The Practice of Godliness by Jerry Bridges. The title describes it well.

Every Man's Battle: Every Man's Guide to Winning the War on Sexual Temptation One Victory at a Time by Stephen Arterburn and Fred Stoeker.

Every Woman's Battle: Discovering God's Plan for Sexual and Emotional Fulfillment by Shannon Ethridge.

Victory over the Darkness by Neil T. Anderson.

Descent into Hell by Charles Williams. Sometimes stories are the most effective way to communicate truth. This book helped me feel the horror and hell of self-centeredness in a way nothing else has. However, this may not be the best Williams book to start with, so try *Many Dimensions*. Charles Williams was one of C.S. Lewis's closest friends, and you will see how deeply his work influenced *That Hideous Strength* (one of my favorite books by Lewis).

The Divine Comedy by Dante Alighieri. Outside of the Bible, I don't know of any book that's as spiritually rich as *The Divine Comedy*.

It has three parts: "Inferno" vividly describes sin and its destructiveness. "Purgatory" is a journey into righteousness. "Paradise" makes me long for God's presence. Be sure to find a good translation with plenty of notes, or you'll be lost. I'm partial to Mark Musa's translation.

Chapter 12: What About Money?

Packing Light: Thoughts on Living Life with Less Baggage by Allison Vesterfelt. This well-written story of Allison's trip around America demonstrates how less can be more.

Neither Poverty nor Riches: A Biblical Theology of Possessions by Craig Bloomberg. An impressive overview of what the Bible has to say about money and possessions. The conclusion alone is worth the price of the book. He also wrote a less technical version, *Christians in an Age of Wealth: A Biblical Theology of Stewardship.*

Money, Possessions, and Eternity by Randy Alcorn.

Thou Shalt Prosper: Ten Commandments for Making Money by Rabbi Daniel Lapin. No, this isn't a "health and wealth" book. Rather, it's a Jewish perspective on what the Bible says about the godliness of making money.

Chapter 14: Between Legalism and Worldliness, Part 2

Gray Matters: Navigating the Space Between Legalism and Liberty by Brett McCracken. This book does a really good job of helping you think critically about what you eat, drink, watch, and listen to. Highly recommended.

Chapter 15: Don't Waste Pain

The Problem of Pain by C.S. Lewis. The classic apologetic book on why God allows pain.

A Grief Observed by C.S. Lewis. This is basically Lewis's journal as he dealt with his wife's death. It gets pretty brutal at some points, but many have found healing in his honesty.

Walking with God Through Pain and Suffering by Tim Keller.

Chapter 16: Hungry for Heaven

The Great Divorce and *The Last Battle* by C.S. Lewis. Both of these stories have helped me feel the reality of heaven.

Surprised by Joy and *The Pilgrim's Regress* by C.S. Lewis. These are both stories of Lewis's conversion. The first is autobiographical and the second is allegorical. In both of them, Lewis describes how God used joy and eternal longings to lead him home.

Phantasies by George MacDonald. This fairy tale changed Lewis's life and fills my heart with a longing for home like nothing else I've read.

Chapter 17: This Life Matters

Surprised by Hope by N.T. Wright. Read it. This is one of the best things you'll find on how much this life and this world matters.

Earthen Vessels: Why Our Bodies Matter to Our Faith by Matthew Lee Anderson.

When Helping Hurts by Steve Corbett and Brian Fikkert. Giving to those in need is not optional, but not all giving is equally helpful. This book will help you understand how to give without harming both giver and recipient.

Walking on Water by Madeleine L'Engle. A great book on the role of art and beauty in the spiritual life.

Sham Pearls for Real Swine by Franky Schaeffer. Written by the son of Francis Schaeffer, this is a harsh criticism of the "state of art" in evangelicalism and a call to do better.

Green like God: Unlocking the Divine Plan for Our Planet by Jonathan Merritt.

Chapter 18: Onward

Radical: Taking Back Your Faith from the American Dream by David Platt. I disagree with Platt on many points, but I love the challenge at the end of his book.

Miscellaneous

The Narnian by Alan Jacobs. This is one of my favorite biographies of all time—so much the better that it's about C.S. Lewis.

Onward by Howard Schultz. The story of how Starbucks grew healthier through a recession.

Notes

Chapter 1: Obsessive and Complacent Christianity

1. C.S. Lewis, *The Weight of Glory: And Other Addresses* (New York: HarperCollins, 2001), 26.

2. Hence the name of his autobiography, *Surprised by Joy.* Joy may not be the best term for it—he also described it as a longing for something beyond this life—but it's no accident that Lewis's enjoyment of this life exceeded that of many Christians I know.

Chapter 3: It's Okay to Be Normal

1. See Wayne Grudem, *Systematic Theology* (Grand Rapids, MI: Zondervan, 1994), pp. 775-77.

2. *Torah* is the Hebrew word for the Pentateuch, the first five books of the Bible.

3. Acts 1:15 says that the believers numbered about 120, but that probably meant all of the Jewish believers in Jerusalem. For instance, we know that many Samaritans and several Gentiles believed in him, but they were not in that room. See Kenneth O. Gangel, *Acts,* vol. 5 of *Holman New Testament Commentary* (Nashville: Broadman & Holman, 1998), p. 12.

4. John 4:4-43, Mark 5:18-19, and Luke 10:38, respectively.

5. C.S. Lewis, *On Learning in Wartime*, chap. 2 in *The Weight of Glory: And Other Addresses* (New York: HarperCollins, 2001), p. 51.

Chapter 4: Honorable Work

1. A handful of New Testament verses are slightly more positive, such as 1 Corinthians 7:1-6 and Hebrews 13:4, but even these pale (or blush?) in comparison to Song of Solomon.

2. Are you worried that your job is incompatible with your faith? Ask yourself...

   • Does the job require you to sin? Can you thrive at your job and honor God at the same time?

   • Do your customers *automatically* sin when they utilize your services? I have friends who install Internet service, but that doesn't make them responsible for the pornography that some customers will download.

- Is the job personally detrimental to you?

If you answered any of those questions yes, you should probably seek some godly counsel and consider getting a new job.

Chapter 5: Greatness for Average Joes

1. See Cal Thomas and Ed Dobson, *Blinded by Might* (Grand Rapids: Zondervan, 1999). Having been deeply involved in conservative politics during the Reagan era, the authors saw firsthand how ineffective politics usually are at creating lasting change.

2. Philippians 2:15-16.

3. 1 Corinthians 6:3.

4. Acts 22:3.

5. John 18:10-18.

6. Frederick Buechner, *Wishful Thinking* (New York: Harper & Row, 1973), p. 95.

7. I first heard this question as part of the Saddleback Church S.H.A.P.E. assessment—a useful tool for finding your calling.

Chapter 6: Why Are Christians So Weird?

1. See Genesis 34:9-10,21-23. Assimilation is precisely what the Shechemites were hoping for.

2. See Genesis 46:33-34.

3. Deuteronomy 22:9-10.

4. Acts 10.

5. Romans 11:13-21; Galatians 3:29.

6. Technically, this statement isn't in the Bible. The expression is a "conflation" (piecing together) of what Jesus said in John 17:11 and verse 16, so the idea is biblical even if the exact wording isn't.

7. This is known as a genetic fallacy, in which a thing (such as Halloween) is judged based on its origins instead of its current meaning or context. Christians make a similar mistake when they say we should call Easter, Resurrection Day because the word Easter supposedly comes from the name of an Anglo-Saxon goddess, Eostre. I assure you, my church doesn't have a single ritual honoring Eostre on Easter. Our fear of pagan origins seriously underestimates God's redemptive power. He has a long history of taking what started out bad and using it to his glory.

Chapter 7: Witnessing Without Weirdness

1. See Tony Kriz, *Neighbors and Wise Men* (Nashville: Thomas Nelson, 2012). Tony reveals that God used a Muslim and atheist (among others) to draw him back from a crisis of faith.

2. Check out these verses:

    healthy relationships—Proverbs 17:1

    provision for family—Proverbs 31:11-22; 1 Timothy 5:8

    fair governments—1 Timothy 2:1-3

    healthy bodies—3 John 3

    long life—Proverbs 16:31

    respect—Proverbs 22:1

3. Ambition is frequently viewed as a bad thing among Christians, yet the Bible encourages it. "Do you see someone skilled in their work? They will serve before kings; they will not serve before officials of low rank" (Proverbs 22:29). The problem isn't with ambition, but selfish ambition (Galatians 5:20).

4. No one is sure where that quote came from, but it may be a misrepresentation of other things he said, such as his statement about preaching with deeds. See his *Rule of 1221,* Article XVII.

5. Peter is writing to Christians who are enduring persecution. How much more should we follow his advice when the worst many of us will endure is being disliked?

Chapter 8: In Defense of Earthly Joys

1. Other synonyms included *enjoy, rejoice, blessed, glad, exult, jubilant, thrill,* and *satisfy.* Christian writers and speakers often differentiate between joy and happiness, but the Bible doesn't make that distinction.

2. The study and an explanation of my methodology can be found on my website, www.Radically Normal.com.

3. These are called the Thanksgiving Psalms. Psalms 65–67 are good examples.

4. See Proverbs 5:18-19 and all of Song of Solomon.

5. For example, see Deuteronomy 16.

6. Proverbs 15:23.

7. Timothy 6:17.

Chapter 9: When God Throws a Party

1. H.G.M. Willamson, *Ezra, Nehemiah,* vol. 16 of *Word Biblical Commentary* (Dallas: Word, 1998), p. 292.

2. Deuteronomy 16:13-15.

3. C.S. Lewis, *Mere Christianity* (New York: Macmillan, 1977), p. 120.

Chapter 10: In Defense of Spiritual Joys

1. This is based on the view that every Sunday is a mini-celebration of the resurrection and that fasting is inappropriate during a celebration.

2. If you've been wounded by bad church experiences, I am truly sorry. That isn't the way it's supposed to be. Church is supposed to be the place where we are loved unconditionally, nurtured, and reminded of God's amazing grace. Take the time you need to heal and seek a healthy church community.

3. These were roughly the lyrics of a song from my youth called "The Greatest Thing," but there are countless of other examples like this.

Chapter 11: Happy Holiness

1. Louis Markos, "Smuggled Theology—Chronicles of Narnia 1," lecture 9 in *The Life and Writings of C.S. Lewis,* The Great Courses: Literature and English Language (The Teaching Company, 2000), download. Lewis and Markos were both well aware that the Puritans were not joyless. Markos was simply using the term as popularly understood.

2. C.S. Lewis, *The Screwtape Letters* (New York: Macmillan, 1961), pp. 101-2.

3. See Ellen Charry, *God and the Art of Happiness* (Grand Rapids, MI: Eerdmans, 2010), part 1.

4. C.S. Lewis, "Weight of Glory," chap. 1 in *Weight of Glory: And Other Addresses* (New York: HarperCollins, 2001), p. 26.

5. C.S. Lewis, *Reflection on the Psalms* (New York: Harvest Books, 1958), p. 30.

6. Mark 9:24.

Chapter 12: What About Money?

1. Read Revelation 18. The description of Babylon sounds uncomfortably like America.

2. For instance, when Paul told the generous Corinthians, "You will be enriched in every way so that you can be generous on every occasion" (2 Corinthians 9:11), he was referring to material as well as immaterial riches. John prayed that Gaius would prosper in all respects (3 John 2). The first Christian convert in Europe, Lydia, was a wealthy merchant. Wealthy Christians provided significantly for the work of the gospel and hosted early church meetings in their houses.

3. See appendix 2 for some good resources on what the Bible says about money.

4. See, for example, Isaiah 58:3,6-7,10.

5. See Luke 12:16-21; James 5:1-6.

6. Proverbs 30:8-9. See also 23:4-5 and 28:20.

7. See Craig Bloomberg, *Neither Poverty nor Riches* (Downers Grove: InterVarsity Press, 2000). Bloomberg points out that God's distribution of the land to the Israelites (Joshua 13–19) and command that land ownership revert back to the original owners every 50 years (Leviticus 25:10-16) prevented Israel from experiencing the widespread extremes of wealth and poverty we see in the world today. But Bloomberg argues against using the Bible to advocate a form of Christian communism.

8. The passages are Luke 18:22 and 12:33, respectively. The Greek word for *everything* (*hosa*) is in 18:22 but not 12:33. God could call someone to give up everything, but that isn't his expectation for every believer.

9. See Proverbs 13:23, Proverbs 19:15, and Deuteronomy 15:11, respectively.

10. 2 Corinthians 8:3-13.

Chapter 13: Between Legalism and Worldliness, Part 1

1. 1 Thessalonians 5:22 KJV.

2. There are some exceptions. For instance, if I'm helping a friend with a pornography addiction, he may need my help to see what fences he should build. And parents need to build fences for their children until they're wise enough to build their own.

Chapter 14: Between Legalism and Worldliness, Part 2

1. F. Wilbur Gingrich and Frederick William Danker, eds., *Shorter Lexicon of the Greek New Testament,* 2nd ed. (Chicago: University of Chicago Press, 1965).

2. Paul makes this clear in 1 Timothy 4:3-5. Some pagan religions taught that the material world is evil and the spiritual world is good, and Paul reacted strongly against this belief.

3. See F.F. Bruce, *1 and 2 Thessalonians,* vol. 45 in *Word Biblical Commentary* (Dallas: Word, 1998), p. 127.

4. Galatians 5:7, Philippians 3:13-14, and 2 Timothy 2:5 are just a few of many examples of Paul's

sporting analogies. First Corinthians 15:33 is a quote from Menander's play *Thais*. Obviously, this doesn't mean Paul agreed with everything that happened at these events.

5. G.F. Hawthorne, Philippians, vol. 43 of *Word Biblical Commentary* (Dallas: Word, 2004), p. 249.

6. Psalm 101:3 also seems to say that we shouldn't look at anything bad, but in the context, David is talking about what kind of person he will allow to serve in his court.

Chapter 15: Don't Waste Pain

1. "It's, however, perhaps more likely that [Jesus's tears] were brought about by the sight of the havoc wrought among people through sin and death in this world." G.R. Beasley-Murray, *John*, vol. 36 of *Word Biblical Commentary* (Dallas: Word, 2002), pp. 193-94.

2. C.S. Lewis, *The Great Divorce* (New York: HarperCollins, 2001), p. 69.

Chapter 16: Hungry for Heaven

1. See 2 Corinthians 5:2 and Romans 8:21.

2. Paul was incredibly close to God, he memorized huge portions of the Old Testament, he was a Christian par excellence, and he had powerful spiritual experiences (including a visit to heaven), yet he continued to feel this hunger.

3. C.S. Lewis, "The Weight of Glory," chap. 1 in T*he Weight of Glory: And Other Addresses* (New York: HarperCollins, 2001), 31.

Chapter 17: This Life Matters

1. I was glad to hear that Starbucks has since implemented a regional recycling policy, so my old store is now recycling.

2. This contrasts with 1 Timothy 4:8, which says it has some value.

3. For instance, passages like Isaiah 65:17-25 describe the new heavens and earth as being something of a return to Eden. "'The wolf and the lamb will feed together, and the lion will eat straw like the ox, but dust will be the serpent's food. They will neither harm nor destroy on all my holy mountain,' says the LORD" (verse 25).

4. The word translated *renewal* is used only twice in the Bible—here and in Titus 3:5, which describes our personal renewal by the Holy Spirit. It was also used by Josephus (Antiquities 11.3.9.66) to describe Israel's return from exile and by Philo (Moses 2.65) to describe the new generation after the flood.

5. To be fair, 2 Peter 3:10 is greatly debated because of some important textual variations, but the NIV, ESV, NRSV, and NET (among others), which follow the oldest copies, support this interpretation.

6. We see this same style of writing in Isaiah 34:4: "All the stars in the sky will be dissolved and the heavens rolled up like a scroll; all the starry host will fall like withered leaves from the vine, like shriveled figs from the fig tree." How can that not be apocalyptic? The heavens are rolled up like a scroll! But in the very next verse we discover that Isaiah is describing God's judgment against Edom, an event that has long since come and gone, with the heavens still in place.

Even though this style sounds strange to our ears, Old Testament prophets frequently describe earthly events using cataclysmic language, and we need to take that into account as we interpret the Bible. The goal of good interpretation is to understand the intended meaning of the authors. For instance, when Isaiah or Peter are being literal (as in 2 Peter 1:16-18), we interpret their words literally. When they're being figurative (as in 2 Peter 2:17—the false teachers are not literally "mists driven by a storm"), we interpret their words figuratively.

7. This is a very brief overview of a much bigger topic. If you want to know more, I highly recommend reading N.T. Wright, *Surprised by Hope* (New York: HarperOne, 2008).

8. C.S. Lewis, *The Last Battle* (New York: Collier Books, 1970), p. 184.

9. Romans 10:14-15, James 1:27, Romans 12:15, and Genesis 1:28, respectively.

10. See Marla Paul, "Religious Young Adults Become Obese by Middle Age," Northwestern University, www.northwestern.edu/newscenter/stories/2011/03/religious-young-adults-obese.html. However, we must remember that correlation does not prove causation.

11. This theory was greatly influenced by the description of heaven in C.S. Lewis's *The Great Divorce* (New York: HarperOne, 2001) and his description of the eldila in *Out of the Silent Planet* (New York: MacMillan 1965).

12. N.T. Wright, *Surprised by Hope* (New York, HarperOne, 2008), p. 208.

Chapter 18: Onward

1. Fredrick Buechner, *Wishful Thinking* (New York: Harper & Row, 1973), p. 95.

More Great Books from Harvest House Publishers

Called to Stay
Caleb Breakey

Will You Stay?

Caleb Breakey prays to God you do.

In *Called to Stay*, Breakey takes a refreshingly honest look at the church, the problem of Millennials leaving, and the stark reality of why the church desperately needs them. He holds nothing back as he unleashes an ambitious rallying cry to heal the church and inject his generation's desire for truth, passion, and conviction into other believers.

Caleb knows that answering the challenge of his own generation leads to a transformed church.

And a changed church can change the world.

Dating Like Airplanes
Caleb Breakey

You've done the online dating thing. You've gone on a hundred blind dates. You've stared slack-jawed at that gorgeous stranger in the coffee shop…and couldn't think of a thing to say. You've scoured the Christian dating advice websites. And you're ready to throw up your hands and be done with romance.

Does meeting your soul mate really need to be this hard?

Stop trying to fall in love, says Caleb Breakey, and start learning how to fly! Just like airplanes soar above the clouds, you can have a relationship that rises above the ordinary and doesn't crash and burn. Caleb, breakout author of *Called to Stay*, traveled his own rocky road to romance, and he'll tell you the truth about courtship and dating, finding your soul mate, and what it really means to pursue Christian relationships. Along the way, you'll discover the greatest romance of all: the love that Christ pours out on you. This is Christian dating advice at its best!

To learn more about Harvest House books and
to read sample chapters, visit our website:

www.harvesthousepublishers.com

HARVEST HOUSE PUBLISHERS
EUGENE, OREGON